Elevate: The Science of Healthy Aging

Maximize Your Potential for Longevity and Well-Being

Pauline Vincent

Table of Contents

INTRODUCTION

In the midst of our busy lives, there's a point where we stop and take a good look at ourselves in the mirror. It's that moment when we notice the changes time has brought—maybe a few more laughter lines etched around our eyes or the hint of silver gracing our hair. We all reach that crossroads where the road ahead seems a bit uncertain, and the map of aging feels like uncharted territory.

Yet, what if I told you that this journey of aging could be not just navigated but mastered? When we look in the mirror, we see not only the subtle changes on our faces, but we also feel the whispers of our bodies and minds nudging us to pay attention. It's a moment loaded with questions. How do we maintain the energy to keep up with life's demands? How do we ensure our mental agility remains sharp? And what about our loved ones, especially our parents, who are starting to face their own health challenges?

These questions are more than mere ponderings; they are the real, everyday concerns that greatly affect every aspect of our lives. As we stand at the intersection of time and aging, we grapple with the pain points that accompany this journey.

For those of us in our 40s and 50s, the struggle is often about not knowing where to start on the fitness journey or how to navigate the nutrition jungle. We've had our share of self-made experiences that never quite turned out as good as we wanted them to be. And then there's the added worry about our parents, watching them navigate their wellness struggles, wondering how we can best support them without encroaching on their independence.

As we enter our 60s and beyond, the quest for guidance becomes more pressing. How do we improve our fitness and mental well-being without the sometimes-embarrassing prospect of a fitness club or a constant reliance on a physiotherapist? The struggle is real, and the need for practical tips and easy-to-follow advice is paramount.

We're at a point where we want to savor every moment, relishing the freedom of retirement and the joys of a life well-lived. But the reality is, the path isn't always clear. We're caught between wanting to maintain our independence and needing a bit of guidance without feeling like we're surrendering to old age.

It's not just about feeling physically fit; it's about maintaining that mental sharpness, that agility that allows us to navigate life's complexities with grace. The desire to remain self-sufficient and vibrant resonates deeply at this stage. We want to enjoy life to the fullest, reveling in the experiences and connections that make each day meaningful.

And for many of us, the thought of diving into a fitness regimen feels intimidating. The idea of sharing a space with gym enthusiasts or committing to rigorous routines can be off-putting. Yet, we crave that energy, that strength to revel in life's adventures.

Moreover, the maze of information out there only adds to the confusion. Sorting through the latest health trends, superfoods, and exercise fads feels like a never-ending expedition without a map.

In this phase, what we truly need is practical advice that acknowledges our stage in life. We need tips that seamlessly integrate into our daily routines, understanding that not everyone wants to spend hours sweating it out in a gym or flipping through pages of complex nutritional charts.

We need guidance that respects our individuality, our desire for autonomy, and our longing for meaningful connections—solutions that don't just focus on physical health but also nourish our mental and emotional well-being, recognizing that holistic wellness isn't a one-size-fits-all concept.

Amidst the overwhelming sea of information, *Elevate: The Science of Healthy Aging* can be your lighthouse, guiding you through the tumultuous waves of health advice and aging myths. It's not just another book but a beacon of clarity and practicality tailored to where you are in life. Rooted in the realms of biohacking and science, it transcends the ordinary boundaries of aging advice, offering strategies to curate a lifestyle that nourishes not only the body, but also the mind and spirit.

By delving into the wisdom woven within these pages, you'll unearth a treasure trove of strategies that transcend the ordinary confines of aging advice. Picture this: waking up each morning invigorated, not just by the absence of bodily aches but by a renewed sense of purpose and vitality.

Through the shared insights, you'll discover the power to curate a lifestyle that nourishes not only your body, but also your mind and spirit. Imagine feeling mentally sharp and agile enough to tackle life's puzzles with ease and clarity. This isn't just about remembering where you left your keys; it's about embracing a cognitive sharpness that fuels your passions and keeps your curiosity alive.

As you navigate the guidance within these pages, you'll find yourself infused with a newfound zest for life. You'll relish the moments, finding joy in the simplest of experiences, and creating a treasure trove of memories that gleam with fulfillment.

This book is more than a roadmap; it's a catalyst for transformation. You'll witness yourself embracing each day with a newfound vigor, exploring opportunities, and relishing the connections that give life its color. It's about savoring the richness of existence—not merely existing, but truly living.

And, perhaps most importantly, it's about reclaiming control over your narrative. No longer confined by societal expectations or aging stereotypes, you'll emerge as the author of your own story—a story brimming with resilience, purpose, and an unwavering enthusiasm for what lies ahead.

Through the wisdom distilled within these pages, your life will become a canvas upon which you paint a masterpiece of wellness and fulfillment. It's not just about aging gracefully; it's about thriving, embracing the art of aging as a masterpiece in its own right.

Now, you might be wondering why you should trust me to be your guide on this transformative journey. Let me share a bit about myself. I'm in my 40s, just like many of you, and not too long ago, I found myself standing at the crossroads of aging, surrounded by a sea of confusing data on how to live a long, powerful, and purposeful life.

As a sports enthusiast who finds solace in the breathtaking beauty of the Alps, I discovered the transformative potential of aging gracefully while navigating the complexities of the hotel industry in Switzerland. However, the turning point for me came with a personal struggle—witnessing the challenges my parents faced.

My mother, in her late 70s, descended into depression after a skiing accident triggered a cascade of health issues. Amidst the maze of medical advice and prescriptions, the essence of her strength and purpose slipped away. I witnessed the pain of cognitive decline and the frustration of misunderstood ailments. Doctors dismissed her struggles as mere consequences of aging, offering little more than antidepressants, which only exacerbated her condition.

Driven by a daughter's love and a quest for answers, I dedicated my time to scientific research on aging. The discoveries were groundbreaking, revealing the transformative power of strength training on brain function, even at the age of 70. Armed with this newfound knowledge, I implemented changes—not just for my mother, but also in my own life.

This book is a culmination of my journey, a guide crafted from personal experience and scientifically proven insights. I understand the frustration of sifting through a flood of information and the difficulty of achieving promised results without the right guidance.

So, as you hold this book in your hands, know that it's more than just a collection of facts and advice. It's a testament to my journey, your potential, and the transformative power that awaits you. If you've ever felt lost in the sea of aging advice, unsure of where to turn, this is the right book for you—a beacon of clarity, practicality, and a promise for a life filled with vitality, purpose, and enthusiasm.

Are you ready to embark on this journey with me? To discover the keys to unlock vitality, mental clarity, and emotional well-being? To create a new narrative of aging that defies limitations and embraces the full spectrum of life's offerings? It's never too late to take control of your narrative and thrive in the art of aging, integrating the science of healthy living, biohacking, and the pursuit of longevity.

If you're seeking a life brimming with vitality, purpose, and enthusiasm, then this is the moment to take that step. Turn the page, and we'll go on this adventure together, embracing the art of aging as a masterpiece in motion.

Chapter 1:

Understanding the Science of

Aging

If you are like me, you have most likely asked this question: What's the secret behind aging gracefully? Why do some people seem to age like fine wine while others feel like they're grappling with time? The answers to these questions lie within the intricate world of the science of aging.

It's time to demystify the aging process, understand the biological and physiological changes that come with it, and discover the key players influencing how we age.

Cellular Aging and Its Impact

Picture your body as a well-orchestrated symphony, where each instrument has its own significant role. Now think about what would happen if some of those instruments started to sound off or even stopped playing altogether. This is similar to the changes our cells go through with aging. Our cells are the foundation of life, and they can experience changes that affect their performance and effectiveness. Over time, these tiny structures become worn out and are unable to divide or replicate any longer.

While it's easy to get caught up in the negatives, let's flip the perspective. Imagine it as your body telling you, "I've had a great run and now I'm going to prioritize quality over quantity." Knowing about cell aging gives us an appreciation for our bodies' strength and inspires us to take good care of ourselves through healthy habits.

The Role of Telomeres

Let's zoom into one fascinating aspect of cellular aging: telomeres. Think of telomeres as the protective caps at the end of our chromosomes, resembling the aglets on the ends of our shoelaces. These tiny structures prevent the fraying and deterioration of genetic information during cell division.

As we age, however, our telomeres naturally shorten. This process acts like a biological clock, influencing the lifespan of our cells. When telomeres become too short, cells can no longer divide, leading to aging-related changes and, eventually, cell death.

Mitochondrial Health

Just as telomeres are like protective caps at the ends of our chromosomes, think of mitochondria as the powerhouse of our cells—a bustling energy hub keeping our bodies running smoothly. These tiny organelles, resembling energetic factories, are fundamental in understanding the aging puzzle.

The Role of Mitochondrial Function

Mitochondria are where the magic happens—they generate the energy essential for cellular function through a process called *oxidative phosphorylation*. However, as we age, these powerhouses experience wear and tear—and this, coupled with accumulated damage from free radicals, compromise mitochondrial function.

Imagine a city facing a power outage—the consequences would be widespread. Similarly, when mitochondrial function declines, our cells struggle to produce adequate energy, affecting various bodily functions. This decline is more than simple fatigue; it plays a pivotal role in age-related diseases and the overall aging process.

Mitochondrial Dysfunction in Age-Related Diseases and Energy-Production Decline

Mitochondrial dysfunction is a key player in the onset and progression of age-related diseases. When these powerhouse organelles falter, it impacts tissues and organs throughout the body. Diseases like Parkinson's, Alzheimer's and cardiovascular problems have been linked to mitochondrial dysfunction. It may not be something you think about every day, but it's actually a really big deal when it comes to the aging process.

Remember how our bodies need energy for repair and maintenance? Well, if there's reduced power being generated from the mitochondria, then we're at risk of accelerated wear and tear on our biological equipment.

Yet, here's the beacon of hope: We have a say in supporting our mitochondria and optimizing their function. Research has indicated that everyday decisions like regular exercise, a nutritious diet loaded with antioxidants, and managing pressure not only affect telomeres but also take on an important part in preserving robust mitochondria.

Understanding the pivotal role of mitochondria in aging opens new avenues for intervention. Scientists are exploring ways to support mitochondrial health, ranging from dietary supplements to novel therapies aimed at rejuvenating these vital energy centers.

So, while the aging process unfolds and mitochondria keep ticking, remember that our actions today shape our tomorrows. By nurturing our mitochondria through lifestyle choices and potentially leveraging upcoming advancements in science, we can actively contribute to aging well.

But here's the silver lining: Lifestyle factors play a significant role in influencing telomere length. Healthy habits, such as regular exercise, a balanced diet, and stress management, have been shown to positively impact cell health. This means that, to a certain extent, we can actively participate in shaping our own aging process.

So, if you're wondering about the secret to aging gracefully, it's not about stopping time; it's about making the most of the time you have. Embracing the science of aging opens the door to a world where our choices matter, where we can optimize our well-being and, in turn, age with vitality.

Epigenetics and Lifestyle: Influences on Gene Expression

Imagine your genes as a library filled with countless books of information about you. Now, epigenetics is like the librarian—it doesn't change the books themselves but decides which ones to bring out, dust off, and read. Understanding this interaction between lifestyle and gene expression opens a fascinating chapter in the story of healthy aging.

Gene Regulation Mechanisms

Epigenetics governs how genes express themselves without altering the underlying genetic code. It's like a symphony conductor, orchestrating which genes play louder or softer, faster or slower. Lifestyle choices and environmental factors influence this conductor, impacting how our genes manifest themselves.

Impact of Diet, Exercise, Stress, and Sleep on Gene Expression and Subsequent Aging

Our daily choices—what we eat, how we move, how we cope with stress, and the quality of our sleep—are not just incidental aspects of life. They are powerful modulators of gene expression, shaping our health trajectory as we age. These are the power players:

- **Diet:** Imagine your diet as the chef crafting a masterpiece. Nutrient-rich foods can activate genes associated with vitality and longevity, while a diet lacking essential nutrients may lead to a discordant symphony within your body.

- **Exercise:** Physical activity, our body's way of rejoicing, triggers a cascade of positive gene expressions. From improving cardiovascular health to boosting mood-regulating genes, exercise is a potent ally in our quest for healthy aging.

- **Stress management:** Chronic stress, on the other hand, can be likened to a dissonant note in our genetic composition. It activates genes associated with inflammation and accelerates the aging process. Conversely, adopting stress-management techniques, whether through meditation or other practices, can harmonize our genetic orchestra.

- **Sleep:** The quality and duration of our sleep influence the genes responsible for repair and rejuvenation. Inadequate sleep disrupts this delicate balance, contributing to premature aging and a host of health issues.

So, here's the revelation: Our genes are not static entities but dynamic players responding to the rhythm of our lives. By understanding and embracing the impact of our daily choices on gene expression, we gain the power to shape our aging process.

The Intersection of Science, Lifestyle, and Aging

As we journey through the intricacies of healthy aging, let's explore a captivating frontier where science, lifestyle, and the aging process converge—the world of our gut microbiota.

Gut Microbiota and Aging: Microbiome and Health

It looks like our gut is home to a ton of microscopic critters, which we collectively call the *gut microbiota*. These tiny occupants have a critical role for us as we age—sort of like guardians of our internal system affecting digestion, immunity, and more. But what makes this microbiome so important?

Also, science is more and more convinced that a calorie is not a calorie, but, rather, how we receive nutrition depends on how healthy our gut microbiomes are. The healthier they are, the more micronutrition can be used from our bodies and there's fewer inflammation risks.

How Does Our Gut Microbiota Influence Immunity, Inflammation, and Cognitive Function?

Regarding aging, these microbial citizens have a tremendous effect on our immune system, inflammation levels, and even cognitive ability in the following ways:

- **Immunity:** It's almost like having your own personal security crew. A balanced gut microbiome helps keep the immune system in check so it knows when it should react correctly or not go overboard with its response. As we get older, this balance is especially significant; an impaired immune system can cause us to be more vulnerable to infections and sickness.

- **Inflammation:** Chronic inflammation often shows up with age-related conditions, but why? The gut microbiota, when balanced correctly, serves as a go-between assisting in keeping inflammation at bay. Conversely, an unbalanced microbiome can add to systemic swelling and hasten the aging process.

- **Cognitive function:** Believe it or not, the gut and intellect are always talking. The gut bacteria affect this chit chat using what's known as the "gut-brain axis." Variations in the intestines' microbiome have been associated with changes in emotionality/moods, cognition, and even dangers of neurodegenerative illnesses.

Gut-Brain Axis

The gut and brain, seemingly distant entities, are intricately connected through a bidirectional communication highway—the gut-brain axis. This axis plays a crucial role in our mental well-being, and its influence on aging is a burgeoning area of scientific exploration.

Consider this axis as a dynamic dialogue between the gut and brain, where the health of one directly affects the other. A healthy gut microbiome supports cognitive function and emotional well-being, contributing to a positive mental outlook as we age.

Biohacking Insights: Techniques for Health Optimization

Let's venture into biohacking—an exciting place where we can tap into optimizing our biology for greater well-being throughout life. Biohacking is a movement that more and more people are exploring and taking their longevity into their own hands.

One of the keys to this big shift lies in comprehending how nutrition affects our genes, providing a pathway for personalizing healthy aging.

Nutrigenomics and Longevity: Understanding Nutrient-Gene Interactions

Nutrigenomics is the science that explores how specific nutrients interact with our genes, influencing gene expression and, consequently, our longevity. Imagine your genes as a finely tuned instrument and nutrients as the melodies that can either harmonize or create discord within this intricate symphony.

Certain nutrients act as powerful signals, turning on genes associated with longevity and vitality. Antioxidants, for example, found abundantly in fruits and veggies, have a huge impact on protecting our cells from oxidative stress as well as slowing the aging process.

Nutrient-Rich Foods and Their Impact on Gene Expression for Healthy Aging

The food we consume is not just fuel; it's information for our genes. Nutrient-rich foods, including colorful vegetables, omega-3 fatty acids, and a variety of antioxidants, send signals that positively influence gene expression. These signals contribute to cellular repair, reduce inflammation, and support overall health.

Consider adopting a rainbow on your plate—a diverse array of fruits and vegetables. Each color represents a unique set of nutrients, each with its own beneficial impact on gene expression. It's not just about eating for today; it's about investing in the longevity of your genetic symphony.

Precision Nutrition

Imagine a nutrition plan tailor-made for your unique genetic composition—this is the promise of precision nutrition. Our genes play a significant role in how our bodies metabolize nutrients, respond to different diets, and age. Precision nutrition aims to harness this information to create personalized strategies for optimal health.

By understanding your genetic profile, you can unlock insights into how your body processes carbohydrates, fats, and proteins. Understanding your genetic profile for precision nutrition involves genetic testing, typically through DNA-testing services. Companies like 23andMe, AncestryDNA, and others offer at-home DNA-testing kits that provide insights into your genetic makeup.

To embark on this journey, simply order a DNA-testing kit, follow the instructions to provide a saliva sample, and send it back to the company. Once your results are available, usually within a few weeks, you'll gain valuable information about how your body processes carbohydrates, fats, and proteins, along with other insights related to health and ancestry.

Armed with this knowledge, you can then seek the guidance of healthcare professionals or certified nutritionists who specialize in interpreting genetic data. They can help you develop a personalized nutrition plan tailored to your unique genetic composition, optimizing your health and well-being.

This knowledge empowers you to make informed choices about your diet, ensuring that it aligns with your genetic predispositions, contributing to a healthier, more vibrant you.

The Emerging Field of Precision Nutrition and Its Role in Aging Gracefully

Precision nutrition is at the forefront of health optimization, representing a paradigm shift in how we approach diet and aging. As this field continues to evolve, we can anticipate more targeted, individualized strategies that empower us to age gracefully and with vitality.

Rejuvenating Therapies and Longevity Science

As we journey deeper into the realm of healthy aging, let's unveil the horizon of rejuvenating therapies and longevity science—an arena where cutting-edge advancements are reshaping our understanding of aging and offering promising avenues for age-related issues.

Regenerative Medicine

Regenerative medicine stands as a beacon of hope in the realm of aging science. Imagine a medical approach not merely focused on managing symptoms but on repairing and regenerating tissues. Stem-cell therapy, a star player in this field, holds the potential to rejuvenate aging cells and tissues. Gene-editing technologies further amplify these possibilities, enabling scientists to target and correct age-related genetic anomalies.

The tantalizing prospect of regenerative medicine lies in its capacity to address the root causes of age-related issues, offering a glimpse into a future where we can reverse, rather than merely cope with, the effects of time.

Anti-Aging Treatments

As science advances, so do our options for interventions that may slow down or reverse the aging process. Anti-aging treatments, backed by rigorous scientific research, are becoming a focal point in the pursuit of extended health span—the period of life spent in good health.

Senolytics, for instance, are emerging as a key player in anti-aging interventions. These treatments target and eliminate senescent cells, which are cells that have ceased to divide, contributing to inflammation and tissue damage. By clearing these cellular "zombies," senolytics aim to promote a more youthful and resilient body. Senolytics, though promising, are primarily in experimental stages, undergoing clinical trials with potential availability through specialized clinics or research studies, rather than mainstream markets.

As we explore the world of age-reversing therapies and longevity science, it's clear that exciting prospects lie ahead. Although these treatments are still in their beginning stages of development, they symbolize a big shift in our approach to aging—which now centers more around not only adding years to lives but also making sure those years have vigor, good health, and zest. Getting rid of old or dysfunctional cells through senolytics interventions might help reduce inflammation, which then could lead us closer toward an extended lifespan.

Emerging Technologies and Biohacking Innovations

In our ever-evolving quest for longevity and vibrant health, emerging technologies and biohacking innovations stand as powerful tools reshaping how we perceive and approach aging. Let's learn about these advancements that are revolutionizing the landscape of proactive aging.

Wearable Devices and Health Monitoring

Enter the era of proactive aging, wherein wearable devices play a pivotal role in monitoring our health parameters in real-time. These smart devices go beyond the traditional functions of step counting; they provide a continuous stream of data, offering insights into various aspects of our well-being.

Today's watches not only tell time but also keep a vigilant eye on your heart rate, sleep patterns, and even stress levels. Wearable tech is becoming a personalized health assistant, empowering individuals to make informed choices for a healthier and more fulfilling life. Investing in a wearable device that tracks your health data empowers you to take control of your well-being, offering valuable insights for informed decisions and proactive steps toward a healthier, vibrant life.

In the upcoming chapters, we'll look into practical techniques, from understanding the impact of intermittent fasting on longevity to exploring the benefits of specific supplements.

Chapter 2:

Nutrition and Vitality

When it comes to the secret sauce of healthy aging, nutrition sits right at the heart of the recipe. Imagine your body as a magnificent castle, and the food you eat as the bricks and mortar that build and sustain it. This chapter covers the vital role of a balanced diet, exploring the magic that happens when you feed your body the right ingredients for a life filled with energy, vibrancy, and longevity.

Introduction to Nutrient-Rich Diets

Macronutrients: The Power Trio

Let's kick things off by talking about the heavy hitters—macronutrients. These are the superheroes of your plate, each playing a unique role in supporting your body's functions.

- **Carbohydrates:** Often given a bad rap, these are your body's preferred source of energy. Think of them as the fuel that keeps your engine running smoothly. Whole grains, fruits, and vegetables are fantastic sources of carbs, providing a steady stream of energy that helps you conquer your day.

- **Proteins:** These are the building blocks of life. Picture proteins as the architects, engineers, and construction workers, repairing and rebuilding your body's cells. Tofu, organic meat, fish, beans, and nuts are all excellent protein sources, helping you maintain muscle mass and vitality.

- **Fats:** Don't be afraid of fats; they're like the cushioning that supports and protects your body. Opt for healthy fats found in avocados, olive oil, and nuts. These not only contribute to heart health but also play a crucial role in maintaining your cells' flexibility and integrity.

Micronutrients: The Secret Agents

Now, let's uncover the secret agents—the micronutrients that operate behind the scenes, ensuring your body functions at its best.

- **Vitamins:** These are the multitaskers of the nutrient world. From boosting your immune system to supporting bone health, vitamins are the unsung heroes. Vitamin-rich foods, including colorful fruits and vegetables, are not just a feast for your eyes but a banquet for your well-being.

- **Minerals:** Think of minerals as the essential ingredients in your castle's foundation, holding it together, keeping it strong. Calcium, for instance, keeps your bones sturdy, while iron ensures your blood is a well-oiled machine. Leafy greens, dairy products, and nuts are your allies in maintaining a robust mineral profile.

A Symphony of Nutrients for Vitality and Longevity

Now that you understand the roles of macronutrients and micronutrients, let's consider the bigger picture—a symphony of nutrients working together to create harmony in your body. It's about appreciating the beauty of balance rather than singling out one nutrient over the other.

Picture your plate as a canvas, and each food group as a stroke of color. Embrace the rainbow, incorporating a variety of fruits and vegetables to ensure a diverse range of nutrients. More than eating, it's about celebrating the abundance of flavors and textures that nature provides.

Let's zoom in on the star players—specific nutrients that act as the guardians of our vitality, helping us age gracefully and joyfully.

- **Antioxidants:** Imagine these as your body's shield against the wear and tear of time. Found abundantly in colorful fruits like berries, and leafy vegetables like kale and spinach, antioxidants combat oxidative stress—the tiny rust that can occur within our cells due to various factors. They're your superheroes, fighting off the effects of aging, promoting radiant skin and a robust immune system.

- **Omega-3 fatty acids:** Omega-3s are like the oil that keeps the gears of your mind turning smoothly. Found in seeds and nuts in general, these fatty acids not only boost cognitive function but also reduce inflammation, easing the stresses that can weigh down our bodies as we age.

- **Vitamins and minerals:** These are the unsung heroes that don't usually get the spotlight they deserve. Take Vitamin D, for instance—it's like the sunshine vitamin, promoting bone health and overall well-being. Minerals like magnesium and potassium are the silent partners in maintaining blood pressure and muscle function. Found in a colorful array of fruits, vegetables, nuts, and seeds, these vitamins and minerals are your allies in the graceful art of aging.

Exploring Anti-Aging Foods

Now, let's venture deeper into the realm of anti-aging foods—a treasure trove of nourishment that not only fuels our bodies but also holds the keys to longevity and vitality.

Think of anti-aging foods as nature's elixirs, brimming with compounds that support our bodies in the quest for longevity. These foods are packed with antioxidants, polyphenols, and a myriad of other nutrients that combat the effects of time, keeping us youthful from within.

The food industry adds sugar to finished products (e.g., jam, sauces, bakery products, the list goes on and on). Beware of No Sugar labels, as almost everything you buy at the supermarket has some sort of sugar in it—read the label.

Sugar comes in many, many forms, such as: sucrose, high fructose corn syrup (HFCS), glucose, fructose, maltose, dextrose, brown sugar, molasses, honey, agave nectar, maple syrup, fruit juice concentrate, cane sugar, coconut sugar, rice syrup, barley malt, beet sugar, corn sweetener, evaporated cane juice, malt syrup, sorghum syrup, treacle, date sugar, panela, rapadura, turbinado sugar, and yellow sugar. Believe it or not, there's more. Always check food labels for hidden sugars. And while there are healthier sugars—called intelligent sugars—the food industry is using almost none of them. These include Tagatose, Galahktose, Isomaltulose, Trehalose, Ribose, Erythritol, and Stevia.

Superfoods for Longevity

- **Berries:** Let's start with the vibrant world of berries— blueberries, strawberries, raspberries, and blackberries. These tiny, colorful jewels are bursting with antioxidants that fight off free radicals, those pesky molecules that can accelerate aging.

- **Dark, leafy greens:** Spinach, kale, and Swiss chard aren't just greens; they're powerhouses of nutrients such as vitamins A, C, and K. These leafy wonders support bone health, aid in collagen production, and promote a glowing complexion.

- **Nuts and seeds:** Walnuts, almonds, chia seeds, and flaxseeds are like tiny packages of goodness. Rich in omega-3 fatty acids, fiber, and antioxidants, they're the snack superheroes that support heart health, brain function, and overall well-being.

- **Turmeric:** This golden spice, often found in curries, contains curcumin—an anti-inflammatory compound that can help reduce the effects of aging on the body.

- **Green tea:** Sip your way to longevity with green tea. Packed with polyphenols and antioxidants, it's been associated with lower risks of heart disease and may even contribute to a longer, healthier life.

Cultures and Longevity

Looking around the globe, we find fascinating case studies in cultures where longevity is not just a wish but a way of life. Take the Okinawans of Japan, for instance. Their diet, rich in vegetables, sweet potatoes, and tofu, has been linked to their exceptional longevity and low rates of age-related diseases.

The Mediterranean diet, celebrated for its emphasis on olive oil, fish, whole grains, and an abundance of fruits and vegetables, has also been associated with improved health and increased lifespan.

Now, let's make these anti-aging superfoods a regular part of our meals, ensuring that we nourish our bodies consistently with the goodness they offer.

Meal-Planning Strategies

1. **Colorful variety:** Plan your meals to include a rainbow of colors. Aim for at least two different colors of fruits or vegetables with every meal. This ensures a diverse range of nutrients, vitamins, and antioxidants.

2. **Weekly superfood showcase:** Designate each week to highlight a specific superfood. Whether it's berries, leafy greens, or nuts,

make it a point to incorporate this superfood into different meals throughout the week.

3. **Preparation and convenience:** Prepare ahead by washing and chopping fruits and vegetables for easy access. Store nuts and seeds in small containers for a quick and convenient snack option.

    o   **Example 1—nutrient-packed vegetable bowl:** Prepare a vibrant vegetable bowl featuring precooked quinoa or whole-wheat pasta as the base, topped with a colorful medley of assorted frozen veggies, a handful of antioxidant-rich frozen berries, and a generous serving of canned beans for added protein and fiber.

    o   **Example 2—wholesome lentil creation:** Craft a wholesome lentil creation by combining precooked lentils with a variety of canned beans, mixing in a selection of prepped vegetables and adding a delightful twist with a side of steamed frozen veggies for a burst of color and nutrition.

Now that we've explored ways to infuse our meals with anti-aging superfoods, let's zoom out and consider the bigger picture—a well-rounded and diverse diet that forms the bedrock of sustained health and longevity.

The "Rainbow Diet"

Imagine your plate as a canvas painted with vibrant hues. The "rainbow diet" emphasizes the importance of incorporating a variety of colorful fruits and vegetables. Each color represents a different set of nutrients and antioxidants. From the reds of tomatoes and peppers to the purples of eggplants and berries, this diverse palette ensures you're getting a wide array of health-promoting compounds.

Balancing Macronutrients

- **Protein:** Ensure a mix of protein sources in your diet. Organic meats, legumes, and tofu offer various amino acids crucial for muscle repair and overall body function. When it comes to meat, opt for organic varieties, where the importance lies in the fact that the animals led a natural life, free from antibiotics and the fast-food culture, which helps contribute not only to your health but also to ethical and sustainable living.

- **Carbohydrates:** Opt for complex carbohydrates like whole grains, vegetables, and fruits. They provide sustained energy, fiber for digestive health, and a plethora of vitamins and minerals. Organic produce minimizes exposure to pesticides, while prioritizing freshness, seasonal, and local options ensures optimal intake of vitamins and minerals. Cooking methods like steaming or roasting preserve micronutrients better than prolonged boiling or frying.

- **Fats:** Include healthy fats from sources like avocados, nuts, seeds, and olive oil. These fats are essential for cell structure, hormone production, and absorption of fat-soluble vitamins.

The Harmony of Nutrients

Balance is the symphony that orchestrates optimal nutrition. It's not just about counting calories or restricting certain food groups; it's about embracing the dance of macronutrients on your plate.

The first priority is any kind of vegetable—raw or steamed, then baked, then cooked, in that order, to maintain nutrients. Berries are the healthiest fruits and best raw. Smoothies are better than convenience or commercial foods, but you will get less fiber in a smoothie than in the whole fruit. Your plate should be ⅔ vegetables and ⅓ protein and/or carbs. Keep in mind that when you eat affects digestion. You want food that's easier to digest in the evening and before bedtime.

Crafting Well-Rounded Meals

- **Mix and match:** Aim for a diverse mix of foods in each meal. Combine proteins, carbohydrates, and fats to create a balanced and satisfying plate.

- **Portion control:** Pay attention to portion sizes to ensure you're getting the right balance of nutrients without overloading your system.

- **Mindful eating:** Listen to your body's cues. Eat slowly, savoring each bite, and stop when you feel comfortably full. Delight in the ritual of mindful eating by consciously chewing each bite around 30 times, savoring the flavors and textures, allowing your body's cues to guide you to contentment.

Achieving a healthy, balanced diet includes flexibility and nourishing your body with a wide array of nutrients.

Intermittent Fasting and Aging

As we continue our journey toward holistic well-being, let's explore a fascinating aspect of nutrition that has gained considerable attention in recent years: intermittent fasting. This practice not only adds a unique dimension to our understanding of aging but also offers potential benefits that go beyond the realm of conventional dietary advice.

Intermittent fasting isn't about *what* you eat but rather *when* you eat. It involves cycling between periods of eating and fasting. It comes in various forms, with two popular methods being:

1. **16/8 method:** This involves fasting for 16 hours a day and limiting your eating window to 8 hours–for example, skipping breakfast and only consuming meals between noon and 8:00 p.m.

2. **5:2 method:** This method involves eating regularly for 5 days a week and significantly reducing calorie intake (usually around 500–600 calories) for the remaining 2 nonconsecutive days.

Scientific Mechanisms

Intermittent fasting triggers a range of cellular processes that support health and potentially slow down the aging process. It promotes autophagy, a cellular cleanup process in which damaged cells are removed and recycled, helping in the renewal of healthy cells.

Additionally, it can enhance hormone function, increase metabolic rate, and improve insulin sensitivity, all of which play vital roles in overall health and aging.

Strategies for Successful Intermittent Fasting

Now that we've uncovered the science behind intermittent fasting and its potential benefits for aging, let's look into practical strategies to help you seamlessly incorporate this lifestyle into your routine. Think of it as a personalized approach to aging gracefully—one fasting window at a time.

Meal-Timing Suggestions and Variations:

- **Start slowly.** If you're new to intermittent fasting, begin with a shorter fasting window–say, 12 hours–and gradually extend it as your body adjusts.

- **Choose your window.** Select a fasting window that aligns with your lifestyle. Whether it's the 16/8 method, the 5:2 approach, or a variation that suits your daily rhythm, find what feels sustainable for you.

- **Hydrate wisely.** Stay hydrated during fasting periods. Water, herbal teas, and black coffee are generally permitted and can help curb hunger.

Addressing Common Challenges

- **Nutrient-rich meals:** Focus on nutrient-dense foods during eating windows to ensure you're getting essential vitamins and minerals. Don't compromise on the quality of your meals.

- **Listen to your body:** Pay attention to hunger cues and adjust your fasting window accordingly. It's essential to find a balance that supports your well-being.

- **Exercise smart:** Plan your workouts during eating windows for sustained energy. However, don't hesitate to listen to your body. When you begin the fasting process, it might seem like fasting affects your exercise performance, but it is better to slowly adjust to it until your body gets used to the fat burning metabolism.

Biohacking Through Diet

In our quest for optimal health and graceful aging, biohacking principles blend seamlessly with dietary practices. Let's look deeper into how we can integrate these techniques into our nutrition, paving the way for personalized approaches that unlock our bodies' potential for well-being.

Biohacking Principles in Nutrition

- **Personalized nutrition based on genetic factors:** Embrace the knowledge gained from genetic testing. This insight allows us to craft nutrition plans tailored to our unique genetic makeup, optimizing our dietary choices for health and vitality.

- **Understanding individual responses with continuous glucose monitors (CGMs):** CGMs offer real-time data on how our bodies respond to different foods. This technology helps us understand individual glucose responses, allowing for personalized meal plans that stabilize blood sugar levels. Understanding individual glucose responses through CGMs is crucial because it empowers us to tailor personalized meal plans, stabilizing blood-sugar levels and preventing excess glucose from being stored as fats in the liver and throughout the body. During insulin-dominant states, our ability to burn and derive nourishment from fats is compromised, which can be critical. Please note that CGMs are not meant for diabetics.

Using Data From Continuous Glucose Monitors (CGMs)

- **Real-time feedback:** CGMs provide insights into how our bodies react to different foods. By analyzing these responses, we can curate meals that maintain stable glucose levels, reducing spikes and crashes.

- **Personalized meal-planning:** Customize your meals based on CGM data. This allows for a tailored approach that optimizes energy levels, supports weight management, and promotes overall well-being.

- **Empowering health through personalized nutrition:** By incorporating biohacking principles into our dietary practices, we're not just eating; we're decoding our bodies' unique language. This personalized approach empowers us to make informed choices that nurture our health and support our journey toward graceful aging.

CGM with Apps and Basic Tests

Now that we've unlocked the potential of biohacking through diet, let's explore how CGMs paired with mobile apps and basic tests can become invaluable tools in our journey toward optimal health and graceful aging. These tools not only provide real-time insights but also empower us to refine our dietary habits for personalized well-being.

Analyzing Data and Making Informed Dietary Decisions

Continuous Glucose Monitors (CGMs)

- **Real-time monitoring:** CGMs offer a continuous stream of data, depicting how our bodies respond to different foods.

- **Identifying patterns:** Analyze glucose trends to identify patterns in your body's response, enabling you to make informed decisions about your dietary choices.

Mobile Apps

- **Data visualization:** Utilize mobile apps designed for CGMs to visualize glucose trends and patterns easily.

- **Meal logging:** Many apps allow you to log your meals, helping you correlate specific foods with glucose responses.

- **Carbs and blood sugar:** By eating various carbohydrates alone and in various combinations, you can test carbohydrates, which are responsible for blood-sugar spikes. Best is to eat them freshly cooked alone, freshly cooked with a lot of veggies, and cold alone. Everybody responds differently to carbs. Another test with the CGM could be how your body react to different orders—

meaning, first eating salad then proteins then carbs, which is generally is the most efficient way to digest.

- **Supersapiens:** Glucose monitoring for athletes.

- **Veri:** Glucose monitoring but with a greater focus on nutrition.

Basic Tests

- **Blood tests:** Periodic blood tests can provide additional insights into nutrient levels, allowing you to fine-tune your diet to address specific deficiencies. You should see your doctor or go to the lab to measure *all* of the markers, including hormones. Try to do this twice a year. It is great inside and if you get into biohacking, you can explore great ways to control our health.

- **Biometric measurements:** Track essential health metrics such as cholesterol levels, blood pressure, and body composition for a comprehensive understanding of your well-being.

Apps and Tools for Biohacking Nutrition

Nutrigenetics Apps

- **DNAfit:** Offers insights into how your genes influence your response to different nutrients, helping you personalize your diet.

- **23andMe:** Provides genetic information that can be used with third-party tools to explore nutrition-related insights.

- **Zoe Nutrition:** Provides personalized nutrition recommendations based on an individual's unique biology and gut health. It helps users make informed food choices to optimize their overall health and well-being. Unfortunately, it is not available in every country, but they also have a good podcast and blog.

Continuous Glucose-Monitoring Apps

- **GlucoseZone:** Not just for monitoring, this app pairs glucose data with tailored exercise programs, providing a holistic approach to managing glucose levels.

Health and Wellness Apps

- **Welltory:** Measures stress and energy levels, aiding in understanding how lifestyle factors impact overall health.

- **Fitbit:** Tracks activity, sleep, and heart rate, offering a holistic view of your well-being.

- **MyFitnessPal:** Allows you to log meals and track macronutrients, providing a comprehensive view of your nutritional intake.

As we embrace the marriage of technology and nutrition, these tools become our allies in the pursuit of optimal health. By analyzing data, making informed choices, and utilizing user-friendly apps, we transform our eating habits into a science—an artful science that aligns with our bodies' unique needs. In the next chapter, we are looking at the benefits of exercise on optimal aging and holistic well-being.

We'll explore the myriad benefits it brings, not only to our physical health but also to our mental and emotional well-being. Together, let's continue this inspiring journey toward a life marked by resilience, vibrancy, and the joyous celebration of our bodies at every stage.

Chapter 3:

Exercise and Energy

In the bustling symphony of life, our bodies play the lead role, and how we move through each act matters more than we often realize. Physical activity is our secret potion, our fountain of youth, the elixir that keeps vitality in our grasp as the years gracefully unfold.

As we embrace the journey of healthy aging, there's one steadfast companion: exercise. Staying active isn't just about fitting into a certain dress size or chasing after an ideal number on the scale; it's about nurturing the incredible machine that is your body, ensuring it remains strong, resilient, and ready to take on the joys of each passing year.

Let's start by unraveling the remarkable connection between physical activity and the maintenance of vitality. Science shows that even when you start doing the absolute minimum of workouts per week, you gain muscle—even in your late 70s. And having good, strong muscles can help with brain function.

Picture this: your body as a finely tuned instrument and exercise as the harmonious melody that keeps it playing sweetly over the years. Engaging in regular physical activity is like giving your body a daily tune-up, helping it navigate the twists and turns of time with grace and resilience. And the best part? You don't need to be a fitness guru to start; you just need the willingness to move and groove in a way that brings you joy.

In this chapter, we'll explore how exercise becomes the secret sauce to maintaining vitality and managing those inevitable age-related conditions. Exercise is the not-so-secret sauce that ensures you're living your life to the fullest, no matter what the calendar says.

Let's talk about the superhero qualities of regular exercise. Imagine it as your secret weapon against the challenges that aging might throw your way.

- **Cardiovascular health:** Your heart, that loyal companion beating rhythmically in your chest, deserves a standing ovation. Regular exercise is like a love letter to your cardiovascular system. It helps improve blood circulation, lowers blood pressure, and reduces the risk of heart disease. Think of it as a heart-boosting symphony, where each step, jog, or dance move contributes to a melody of health.

- **Muscle strength:** Strong muscles are the unsung heroes of graceful aging. They provide support to your bones, help you maintain good posture, and make everyday tasks feel like a breeze. With the right exercises, you can sculpt your muscles and enjoy the freedom of movement that allows you to savor life's precious moments without feeling restricted.

- **Bone density:** Aging doesn't have to equate to fragile bones. Through weight-bearing exercises like walking, dancing, or lifting light weights, you can enhance bone density, reducing the risk of osteoporosis. Let's build a solid foundation for your bones that withstands the test of time. Weight-bearing exercises stimulate the bones to become denser and stronger. It's like giving your bones a workout, encouraging them to be robust and resilient. So, lace up those sneakers, turn up the music, and let the rhythm be your guide to stronger, more resilient bones.

- **Mental well-being:** Now, let's shift our focus to the powerhouse above your shoulders—your brain. Exercise isn't just about the body; it's a mental symphony that elevates your mood, sharpens your focus, and keeps the blues at bay. When you move, your brain releases endorphins, those delightful neurotransmitters that make you feel like you're dancing on clouds. Say goodbye to stress and hello to a brighter, more positive outlook on life.

- **Flexibility and balance:** Picture a ballet dancer gracefully moving across the stage. While you may not aspire to pirouette, incorporating exercises that enhance flexibility and balance into your routine is a game-changer. As we age, maintaining flexibility helps prevent injuries, while improved balance ensures you're striding through life with confidence and poise. Yoga, tai chi, or simple stretching exercises can be your allies in this endeavor.

Age-Related Challenges

Let's address the common challenges individuals face as they gracefully age and how exercise can be the ultimate antidote.

- **Joint stiffness:** Ever felt a little creakiness when getting out of bed? Joint stiffness is a common companion on the journey of aging. But fear not! Regular movement, especially exercises that focus on joint mobility, can lubricate those hinges and keep you moving smoothly. Think of it as oiling the gears of a well-loved machine, ensuring it operates with ease.

- **Decreased metabolism:** Metabolism, the engine that fuels your body, tends to slow down with age. But here's the good news: Exercise stokes the metabolic flames. It helps you maintain a healthy weight, boosts energy levels, and supports overall well-being. So, lace up those sneakers, and let's kickstart that metabolism together.

- **Reduced energy levels:** Feeling like your energy tank isn't as full as it used to be? Exercise might just be the jumpstart your body needs. Counterintuitive as it may seem, moving your body can actually boost your energy levels. By engaging in regular physical activity, you're enhancing your body's efficiency in using oxygen and nutrients, leading to increased energy reserves. It's like recharging your batteries with each step and stretch.

- **Emotional well-being:** As life unfolds, emotional well-being becomes a cherished asset. Exercise isn't just a physical activity; it's a potent mood enhancer. It combats feelings of anxiety and depression, fostering a positive outlook on life. Those feel-good endorphins released during exercise? They're your companions in navigating the emotional ebbs and flows of life.

Tailored Exercises for Different Fitness Levels

Now that we've established the incredible emotional benefits of exercise, let's look at making movement accessible for everyone. Fitness isn't a one-size-fits-all journey, and the beauty lies in finding what feels right for you.

1. **Gentle start for beginners:** If you're just starting your fitness journey, fear not! Begin with low-impact exercises such as walking, swimming, or gentle yoga. These activities are kind to your joints, allowing you to build strength and stamina gradually. The key is to listen to your body and progress at a pace that feels comfortable.

2. **Intermediate adventures:** For those who've been flirting with exercise for a while, it's time to add a bit of spice. Incorporate activities like brisk walking, cycling, or group fitness classes. Challenge yourself, but always honor your body's signals. Remember, it's not about perfection but about progress and enjoyment.

3. **Advanced adventures:** For the fitness enthusiasts seeking an extra dose of challenge, the world is your playground! Engage in activities such as running, weight training, or high-intensity interval training (HIIT). These exercises can elevate your heart rate and push your boundaries, all while sculpting your body and boosting those endorphins.

4. **Adaptability for all:** There's no "right" way to exercise, only what's right for you. Modify any exercise to suit your comfort

level and health considerations. If an activity doesn't resonate with your body, find alternatives that do. The goal is inclusivity, embracing the joy of movement at every fitness level.

Age-Neutral Fitness

Let's shatter the notion that exercise should conform to age brackets. Age-neutral fitness is the anthem here, celebrating the idea that exercise should cater to individual abilities rather than arbitrary numbers.

- **Listen to your body.** Your body is your compass. It knows your limits and capabilities better than any fitness trend or number on your birth certificate. Pay attention to how you feel during exercise. If it feels good, keep going. If it doesn't, honor your body's cues and modify accordingly.

- **Adapt and modify.** Every body is unique, and that's the beauty of it. Embrace modifications and adaptations that suit your needs. If a particular exercise doesn't feel right, there's always a variation that can offer similar benefits without strain.

- **Progress at your own pace.** The journey to fitness isn't a race against time; it's a celebration of your progress. Don't compare your journey to someone else's. Focus on your growth, no matter how small the steps may seem. Each step forward is a victory in itself.

Age-neutral fitness embodies the essence of embracing your body's strengths and respecting its limitations. It's about honoring your individuality while celebrating the joy of movement.

Goal-Setting

Now that we've immersed ourselves in the liberating world of age-neutral fitness, let's take a moment to harness the power of goal-setting. Goals are like guiding stars, illuminating your fitness journey and transforming it into a purposeful adventure. Embrace the idea that your goals are as unique as your fingerprints–personal, distinctive, and tailored to your aspirations.

- **Long-term aspirations:** Imagine yourself a year from now, two years, or even in your 80s. What kind of vibrant, energized individual do you aspire to be? Envision your future self, radiating health, strength, and boundless vitality. These long-term aspirations form the foundation of your fitness journey, providing direction and motivation.

- **Immediate abilities:** While long-term goals paint a compelling vision of the future, don't forget the beauty of the present moment. What can you achieve today, this week, or this month? Set immediate goals that align with your current abilities and gradually build upon them. It's not about the destination; it's about savoring each step of the journey.

- **Goals:** Your fitness goal should have at least two components: cardiovascular health and strength. Your goals should target both points. If you consider flexibility and balance as a goal, congratulations! This is also a very good goal, but not in the minimum range.

- **Celebrate progress:** Remember, every step forward is a victory. Celebrate your progress, no matter how small it may seem. Did you increase your daily step count? Celebrate! Did you hold that yoga pose a few seconds longer? Celebrate! Acknowledging your achievements fuels motivation and instills a positive mindset, adding joy to your fitness journey.

- **Adapt and evolve:** Goals are not set in stone; they're flexible, just like you. As you evolve physically and mentally, so should your goals. Don't hesitate to adapt and tweak them based on your changing needs and aspirations. Your goal should be to keep the journey dynamic and infused with a sense of purpose.

Fitness: The Blueprint for Healthy Aging

As we continue our exploration of age-neutral fitness, let's check out the concept of functional fitness—the ultimate blueprint for healthy aging. Functional fitness should make you feel good—it's about cultivating the strength, agility, and balance needed to lead a vibrant and independent life at any age.

Fitness at 70+, 80+

Age is a badge of honor, a testament to resilience and wisdom. Fitness at 70+ and 80+ isn't about extreme feats but about cherishing movement that sustains a fulfilling life.

- **Strength:** For individuals in their 70s and 80s, maintaining strength is pivotal for independence and vitality. Activities like bodyweight exercises, resistance bands, or gentle weightlifting can help preserve muscle mass, supporting daily tasks and reducing the risk of falls. Strength is also essential for brain function.

- **Agility:** As the years gracefully advance, agility becomes a cherished ally. Incorporate exercises that enhance balance, coordination, and flexibility. Tai chi, yoga, or simple balance drills can fortify stability, ensuring you move through life's moments with grace and confidence.

- **Balanced approach:** A holistic approach to fitness is the golden key. Embrace a balanced routine that includes aerobic activities, strength-training, flexibility exercises, and mindful practices.

This comprehensive blend nurtures overall well-being, catering to the diverse needs of your body and mind.

Remember, these fitness plans aren't rigid blueprints but flexible guides that honor individual capabilities and preferences. They're invitations to embrace movement that enriches life, ensuring that every day is lived with vitality and purpose, regardless of age.

Reverse-Engineering Fitness

Embarking on a fitness journey is like setting sail on a personal odyssey, and the compass guiding your ship is none other than your own goals. Let's unravel the art of reverse engineering fitness—a process that enables you to understand where you are, where you want to go, and the exciting steps to bridge that gap, regardless of your age.

1. **Assess your current fitness level.** Begin by taking stock of where you are. Assess your strengths, identify areas that need attention, and recognize your current fitness baseline. Are you a seasoned fitness enthusiast or just starting the journey? Every journey is unique, and acknowledging your starting point is the first step toward progress.

2. **Define your fitness goals.** What does fitness success look like to you? Define your goals with clarity and specificity. Whether it's increasing stamina, building muscle strength, improving flexibility, or a combination of these, having a clear vision empowers your journey. Your goals are the stars guiding you through the fitness galaxy.

3. **Break down your goals.** Reverse engineering is about breaking down large goals into manageable steps. Let's say your goal is to improve cardiovascular health. Break it into smaller tasks like starting with a 10-minute daily walk and gradually increasing the duration. These smaller steps make your journey less daunting and more achievable.

4. **Identify necessary steps.** Each goal has a set of actions that will lead you there. If your aim is increased flexibility,

incorporating daily stretching exercises or joining a yoga class could be essential steps. These steps become your roadmap, guiding you through your fitness journey.

5. **Listen to your body.** As you embark on this journey, your body becomes your compass. Listen to its cues and adjust your steps accordingly. If an exercise feels too strenuous, consider modifications. If it feels invigorating, perhaps it's time to take a small leap forward. The art of listening transforms your fitness journey into a harmonious dance with your body.

6. **Celebrate milestones.** Every step forward is a milestone, a testament to your dedication and resilience. Celebrate these victories, no matter how small. Whether it's reaching a new fitness level, holding a challenging yoga pose, or consistently sticking to your routine—each achievement is a badge of honor on your fitness expedition.

Reverse-engineering fitness is an empowering process that turns your aspirations into actionable steps. It transforms your fitness journey from a distant dream into a tangible reality. As you navigate through each step, remember that this journey is uniquely yours, and every effort brings you closer to the vibrant, healthy, and empowered version of yourself.

Fitness Routines

As we look more closely at the heart of your fitness journey, let's explore the dynamic realm of fitness routines. These are not just exercises; they are purposeful movements that enhance your everyday life, fostering strength, agility, and vitality.

Strength and Resistance

- **The foundation of strength:** Strength is the bedrock of fitness, especially as we gracefully age. Incorporate strength-training routines that target major muscle groups—legs, arms, back, and core. Simple bodyweight exercises like squats, lunges, and push-ups lay a solid foundation, fostering overall strength and stability.

- **Resistance training:** Resistance training adds an exciting dimension to your strength repertoire. Whether it's using resistance bands, free weights, or gym machines, these exercises challenge your muscles, promoting growth and enhancing your metabolic rate. The magic lies in the controlled resistance, fostering muscle endurance and vitality.

Weeks 1–4: Establishing the Foundation

Monday and Thursday

- **Bodyweight squats:** 3 sets of 12–15 repetitions

- **Push-ups (wall or modified):** 3 sets of 10–12 repetitions

- **Planks:** 3 sets, holding for 30 seconds each

Tuesday and Friday

- Walking or light jogging: 20–30 minutes

- Resistance-band exercises: 3 sets of bicep curls and triceps extensions, 12–15 repetitions each

Wednesday and Saturday

- Rest day or light stretching/yoga for recovery

Sunday

- **Leisurely activity of your choice:** A nature walk, gardening, or a gentle bike ride

Weeks 5–8: Introducing Resistance

Monday and Thursday

- **Weighted squats:** 3 sets of 10–12 repetitions

- **Chest press with dumbbells or resistance bands:** 3 sets of 12–15 repetitions

- **Planks with alternating leg lifts:** 3 sets, holding for 30 seconds each

Tuesday and Friday

- **Interval training:** 20 minutes (alternating between brisk walking and light jogging)

- **Resistance-band exercises:** 3 sets of rows and lateral raises, 12–15 repetitions each

Wednesday and Saturday

- **Active recovery:** Light stretching, yoga, or a leisurely swim

Sunday

- **Enjoy a longer, moderate-intensity activity:** A scenic hike, a bike ride, or a dance class

Endurance Cardio and HIIT

When it comes to healthy aging, cardiovascular health takes center stage. These dynamic exercises are not just about breaking a sweat; they're a celebration of your heart's vitality and resilience.

Benefits of Endurance Training

- **Heart health:** Endurance cardio, whether it's brisk walking, cycling, or swimming, is a love letter to your heart. These activities elevate your heart rate, strengthen your cardiovascular system, improve blood flow, and reduce the risk of heart disease. It's like giving your heart a rhythmic dance to keep it happy and healthy.

- **Increased stamina:** As we age, maintaining stamina becomes paramount for embracing life's adventures. Endurance training gradually builds your stamina, allowing you to engage in activities with vigor and enthusiasm. Whether it's a leisurely stroll through nature or an energetic dance class, increased stamina enhances the joy and spontaneity of daily living.

- **Weight management:** Endurance cardio is a fantastic ally in the battle against weight gain. These exercises burn calories, helping you maintain a healthy weight. Additionally, they contribute to a more efficient metabolism, making it easier to manage weight and body composition.

Occasional HIIT for a Burst of Energy

- **Boosted metabolism:** HIIT, with its alternating bursts of intense exercise and short recovery periods, is like a metabolic boost. It elevates your metabolism, encouraging your body to continue burning calories even after the workout. It's an efficient way to amplify the benefits of exercise in a shorter time frame.

- **Improved cardiovascular fitness:** Despite its intensity, HIIT can be adapted to various fitness levels. It challenges your cardiovascular system, enhancing its efficiency and promoting better oxygen utilization. This translates into improved cardiovascular fitness, endurance, and overall heart health.

- **Time-efficient workouts:** For those with busy schedules, HIIT is a superhero. These workouts are short, intense, and effective, making them ideal for individuals with time constraints. In just a fraction of the time, you can reap the rewards of a full-body workout that leaves you invigorated.

  Fact: You can increase your pulse for a short period of time, every or every other time, when you do a strength or endurance workout. This has the same effect as a whole HIIT session.

Recommended Frequency and Intensity for Aging Individuals

Endurance Cardio

- **Frequency:** Aim for at least 150 minutes of moderate-intensity aerobic activity per week, or 75 minutes of vigorous-intensity activity–or a mixture of both, but the low heart rate is the more important part–spread throughout the week.

- **Intensity:** Maintain a pace that elevates your heart rate but allows you to carry on a conversation. You should feel challenged but still in control.

HIIT

- **Frequency:** Max. 1 session per week, or a minimum of 3 times bringing up the heart rate for a short time (1 minute) in your normal training.

- **Intensity:** Tailor the intensity to your fitness level. Beginners can start with shorter intervals and longer rest periods, gradually progressing as stamina improves.

Regeneration and Recovery Practices

In the mosaic of fitness, regeneration and recovery are the soothing notes that harmonize the symphony of movement. Let's explore the serene realms of mind-body practices like yoga and tai chi—ancient arts that not only nurture physical recovery but also bestow tranquility upon the mind and spirit.

Mind-Body Practices for Recovery

- **Yoga's healing embrace:** Yoga is more than just a series of poses; it's a graceful dance between body, breath, and mind. Its gentle stretches and postures promote physical recovery by alleviating muscle tension and improving flexibility. As you flow through asanas (poses) and synchronize your breath, yoga becomes a haven for relaxation, calming the nervous system and reducing stress.

- **Tai Chi's fluidity and balance:** Tai Chi, often referred to as a moving meditation, is a dance of serenity and balance. Its slow, deliberate movements enhance physical recovery by promoting joint mobility, stability, and balance. As you engage in the rhythmic flow of Tai Chi, it becomes a meditative practice that soothes the mind, fosters inner calmness, and reduces anxiety.

Benefits of Yoga and Tai Chi

- **Physical recovery:** Both yoga and Tai Chi offer gentle movements that aid in the recovery of muscles, improve flexibility, and support joint health. They're like therapeutic massages for the body, easing tension and enhancing recovery after more intense workouts.

- **Stress reduction:** The magic of these mind-body practices lies in their ability to calm the mind. Through mindful breathing and intentional movements, they reduce cortisol levels (the stress hormone) and induce a state of tranquility, fostering a sense of peace amidst life's hustle and bustle.

- **Mental well-being:** Yoga and Tai Chi are sanctuaries for mental well-being. They encourage mindfulness, allowing you to be present in the moment, letting go of worries and anxieties. This mental clarity promotes a sense of balance, resilience, and an overall feeling of inner harmony.

Incorporating Yoga and Tai Chi Into Your Routine

Yoga

- Start with beginner-friendly classes or online sessions focusing on gentle yoga or restorative yoga.

- Aim for at least 2–3 sessions per week, gradually increasing frequency as you feel comfortable.

- Focus on deep, mindful breathing and gentle stretches that promote relaxation.

Tai Chi

- Consider joining a Tai Chi class or finding online resources offering introductory sessions.

- Begin with simple, slow movements, focusing on proper form and breathing.

- Aim for 2–3 sessions per week, gradually building consistency and incorporating more complex movements.

As you embrace the healing grace of yoga and Tai Chi, remember that these practices aren't just about physical recovery; they're about nurturing your mind and spirit. They're invitations to find solace in movement, to breathe deeply, and to cultivate a sanctuary of serenity within yourself. Each pose, each graceful movement becomes a melody of rejuvenation, soothing both body and soul.

Incorporating Mind-Body Recovery

In the fast-paced dance of life, finding moments of stillness and serenity is a gift you give to yourself. Let's explore practical ways to seamlessly weave mind-body practices like yoga and Tai Chi into your daily routines, creating pockets of tranquility that serve as anchors for recovery.

1. **Morning mindfulness:** Kickstart your day with a gentle yoga or Tai Chi routine. This can be as short as 10–15 minutes, offering a mindful transition from sleep to wakefulness. Engaging in these practices in the morning sets a positive tone for the day, promoting mental clarity and physical well-being.

2. **Midday rejuvenation:** Amidst the demands of the day, steal a few moments for a mindful break. It could be a short yoga stretch at your desk, a brief Tai Chi session in a quiet corner, or even a mindful breathing exercise. These microbreaks recharge your mental energy, enhance focus, and ease physical tension.

3. **Lunchtime serenity:** Lunch breaks are perfect opportunities for mind-body recovery. Find a quiet space, indoors or outdoors, and indulge in a gentle yoga flow or a few Tai Chi movements. Not only does this aid digestion, it also provides a serene interlude, allowing you to return to your tasks with renewed vigor.

4. **Evening unwind:** As the day winds down, gift yourself a moment of restoration. Engage in a more extended yoga or Tai Chi session, focusing on gentle stretches and relaxation. This

serves as a beautiful transition from the demands of the day to a peaceful evening, preparing your body and mind for restful sleep.

5. **Mindful transitions:** Integrate mind-body practices into transitional moments. Instead of scrolling through your phone or rushing through tasks, pause for a few minutes of mindful breathing, a brief yoga pose, or a Tai Chi movement. These intentional pauses create islands of calm in the midst of life's currents.

6. **Weekend retreats:** Weekends offer a chance to try more mind-body practices. Set aside time for longer yoga sessions or immerse yourself in the flowing movements of Tai Chi. This becomes a ritual of self-care, nurturing your body, mind, and spirit for the week ahead.

7. **Social serenity:** Transform social moments into opportunities for mind-body recovery. Consider joining a friend for a yoga class or inviting a loved one to explore Tai Chi together. Shared practices deepen connections and infuse moments of joy and serenity into your relationships.

Remember, the key is not to view mind-body practices as additional tasks but as necessary for your daily health and serenity. By seamlessly integrating these moments of recovery, you cultivate a holistic approach to well-being—one where tranquility and vitality coexist harmoniously. These practices are not obligations; they are gifts you offer to yourself, fostering a life where every breath is a celebration of balance and restoration.

Optimal Recovery Frequency

Recovery isn't a luxury; it's an essential component of a sustainable and vibrant fitness journey. Let's navigate through the optimal frequency and duration necessary for effective recovery, acknowledging the individuality of needs and the adaptable nature of well-being.

Minimum Requirement for Effective Recovery

Recovery isn't a one-size-fits-all equation. However, certain minimum guidelines can serve as foundational pillars:

- **Duration:** Aim for a minimum of 7–9 hours of quality sleep per night. Sleep is a fundamental aspect of recovery, aiding in muscle repair, hormone regulation, and overall rejuvenation.

- **Frequency:** Incorporate at least 1–2 rest days per week into your fitness routine. These days allow your body to recover and rebuild, preventing burnout and reducing the risk of overuse injuries.

Individual Differences and Adaptability

- **Listen to your body:** Your body is an eloquent communicator. Pay attention to its cues. If you feel unusually fatigued, sore, or experience persistent discomfort, it might signal the need for additional recovery time.

- **Adapt to activity intensity:** High-intensity workouts or prolonged vigorous activities might necessitate more frequent recovery periods. Conversely, low-impact activities might require less recovery time.

- **Age and fitness level:** Individual differences based on age, fitness level, and health conditions play a significant role. Older individuals might require slightly longer recovery periods compared to younger counterparts. Additionally, someone new to fitness might need more recovery than a seasoned athlete.

- **Stress and lifestyle factors:** External stressors, work demands, and lifestyle factors can impact recovery needs. During times of heightened stress, focusing on adequate recovery becomes even more crucial for overall well-being. Sickness or any kind of inflammation is a huge stress factor as well, even if you do not recognize it.

Adaptability and Fluidity in Recovery

- **Flexibility in planning:** Embrace a flexible approach to recovery. If your body signals the need for more rest, adapt your schedule accordingly. It's not about sticking strictly to a regimen but responding intuitively to your body's needs.

- **Active recovery:** Incorporate active recovery strategies on rest days. This might include gentle activities like walking, light stretching, or engaging in mind-body practices like yoga or Tai Chi, which promote blood flow and aid in muscle recovery without intense strain.

- **Hydration and nutrition:** Optimal recovery extends beyond rest; it involves hydration and nourishment. Ensure you're adequately hydrated and consuming a balanced diet rich in nutrients that aid in recovery, such as protein and antioxidants.

Seeking Optimal Recovery

Identifying and implementing optimal recovery practices is akin to crafting a personalized symphony of rejuvenation—it's a melody that harmonizes with your body's unique rhythms and needs. Let's explore strategies to navigate this path and curate recovery practices tailored to individual well-being.

Self-Awareness and Reflection

- **Listen intuitively.** Cultivate self-awareness by tuning in to your body's signals. Take moments throughout the day to check in with yourself. Are you feeling fatigued? Sore? Restless? These cues guide you toward understanding your body's recovery needs.

- **Reflect on responses.** After workouts or periods of intense activity, reflect on how your body responds. Do you recover quickly, or does it take longer than usual? You can measure the pulse and how quickly it goes down to 100 (when you've taken it up to around 150). If you are very fit, it takes less than a minute; if you need more recovery time, it takes longer. This reflection helps identify patterns and informs future recovery strategies. It is also important to note that the pulse lowers faster when you are recovered and comes with a happy feeling as an added benefit.

Individualized Recovery Techniques

- **Sleep hygiene:** Prioritize quality sleep. Establish a sleep routine, create a comfortable sleep environment, and practice relaxation techniques before bedtime to optimize rest. And if you are lucky enough to be able to nap during the day, it's also a good recovery method.

- **Nutrition and hydration:** Fuel your body with nutritious meals and stay adequately hydrated. Foods rich in protein, antioxidants, and healthy fats aid in recovery. Hydration supports optimal bodily functions.

- **Active recovery:** Experiment with various forms of active recovery, such as light stretching, foam rolling, or engaging in low-intensity activities like walking or cycling. These aid in muscle recovery and promote blood flow without causing additional strain.

Recovery Protocols and Schedules

- **Periodization:** Incorporate periods of active training and deliberate recovery into your fitness schedule. Periodization allows for structured recovery phases, preventing burnout and promoting long-term progress.

- **Micro-recovery:** Integrate micro-recovery strategies throughout the day. Take short breaks during work or intensive activities for brief stretches or deep-breathing exercises to alleviate tension and recharge.

- **Maxi-recovery:** Every 3 months, or longer, of a continuous fitness routine, take a larger break of 7–10 days solely for recovery and wellness activities.

Trial and Adaptation

- **Experiment and assess.** Try different recovery practices and observe their impact on your well-being. Does a particular recovery technique leave you feeling refreshed and rejuvenated? Or does it cause additional strain? Assess the effectiveness of each strategy and adjust your practice accordingly.

- **Adapt based on feedback.** Based on your assessment, refine your recovery strategies. Discard what doesn't work and embrace what resonates. It's an ongoing process of fine-tuning based on your body's responses.

Professional Guidance and Support

- **Consult experts.** Seek guidance from fitness professionals, coaches, or healthcare providers. They can offer insights tailored to your specific needs, helping design personalized recovery plans aligned with your goals and limitations.

Optimal recovery is a voyage of self-discovery—an exploration of what best nourishes and revitalizes your body and mind. By embracing a curious and attentive mindset, you unlock the door to a treasure trove of recovery practices uniquely suited to your well-being.

Biohacking Techniques in Fitness

In the era of wellness innovation, biohacking has emerged as a dynamic approach to optimizing fitness, leveraging science and technology to enhance human performance. Next we'll learn about cutting-edge fitness technologies and explore innovative solutions that propel us into the future of well-being.

Cutting-Edge Fitness Technologies

Wearable Tech:

- **Smart fitness trackers:** These devices are more than stylish accessories– they monitor key metrics such as heart rate, steps taken, sleep quality, and even stress levels through heart-rate variability. Real-time feedback empowers users to make informed decisions about their fitness routines and recovery.

- **Smartwatches:** Beyond telling time, smartwatches are fitness command centers. They track workouts, monitor health metrics, and provide personalized insights. Some models even offer ECG and blood-oxygen-level monitoring, bringing clinical-grade data to your wrist.

- **Biometric apparel:** Imagine fitness clothing embedded with sensors that measure muscle activity, posture, and other physiological parameters. Biometric apparel offers a nonintrusive way to gather data, giving users a comprehensive understanding of their body's responses to exercise.

AI-Driven Workout Programs

- **Personalized virtual trainers:** AI algorithms analyze your fitness data to create customized workout plans. These plans adapt based on your progress and feedback, ensuring that each session is optimized for your goals and capabilities.

- **Interactive fitness apps:** Apps powered by AI guide users through workouts, offering real-time feedback on form, intensity, and pacing. This interactive coaching experience brings the expertise of a personal trainer into the convenience of your home.

Innovative Solutions

Virtual and Augmented Reality (VR/AR)

- **Immersive fitness experiences:** VR and AR technologies transport users to virtual landscapes for their workouts. Whether cycling through scenic routes or participating in interactive fitness games, these experiences make exercise engaging and enjoyable. Keep in mind that these can be very addictive!

Recovery Tech

- **Cryotherapy devices:** Cryotherapy involves exposing the body to extremely cold temperatures for short periods. Portable cryotherapy devices allow individuals to target specific areas, reducing inflammation and accelerating muscle recovery.

- **Compression therapy:** Compression sleeves and boots use pneumatic compression to enhance circulation, reduce muscle soreness, and expedite recovery. These devices are popular among athletes and fitness enthusiasts for post-workout recovery.

- **Red-light therapy:** Also known as *photobiomodulation*, red-light therapy is a noninvasive treatment that uses red-light wavelengths to stimulate cellular function and promote healing, reducing inflammation and improving skin health. There are all kinds of devices on the market.

- **Hydrogen water:** The main benefit of hydrogen water is its potential as an antioxidant, which means it may help reduce oxidative stress in the body. However, further research is needed to fully understand and confirm these potential benefits.

Biometric Feedback

- **Heart rate variability (HRV) monitors:** HRV monitors assess the variation in time between heartbeats, offering insights into the autonomic nervous system. This data helps users gauge their readiness for intense workouts and provides valuable information on stress levels.

- **Blood glucose monitoring:** Traditionally associated with diabetes management, continuous glucose monitors are now used by fitness enthusiasts to understand how different foods and activities impact blood glucose levels, optimizing nutrition and performance. See Chapter 2 for more.

The marriage of fitness and technology opens doors to a realm of possibilities, empowering individuals to approach their well-being with unprecedented precision and personalization. As we embrace these biohacking techniques, we embark on a journey where the intersection of science and fitness propels us toward a future of optimized health and performance.

Chapter 4:

Managing Stress and Mental Well-Being

Aging is an incredible journey, marked by experiences that shape us and memories that enrich our lives. But let's talk about a constant companion on this journey: stress. It's like that unwelcome guest who always seems to show up uninvited. But here's the thing: Understanding stress is key to unlocking the secrets of healthy aging.

Picture this: Our bodies are like finely tuned machines, bustling with an intricate system of gears and cogs. But just like any machine, excessive strain and wear and tear can gradually take a toll, impacting how it operates over time. Stress is one of those factors that can grease the wheels or jam the gears in our journey of aging. Imagine two cars parked by the ocean—one pristine, shielded from the salty breeze, the other constantly battered by the sea spray. The one near the ocean represents someone immersed in a stress-inducing environment, perhaps work pressures or family demands. This car needs more care, more frequent checks, and rust protection to weather the salty onslaught.

Similarly, people often view stress as solely caused by their environment—an external force they have no control over. But here's the revelation: Stress isn't just about what's around us; it's about how we respond to it. The person near the ocean might need more care, but they can also learn ways to shield themselves, reducing the impact of the saltwater.

Just as a car owner near the ocean must take extra measures to protect their vehicle, we must actively counteract the effects of stress. It's about realizing that stress isn't just something that happens to us; it's a two-way street. We have the power to influence our stress levels, to become the drivers navigating the road of our well-being.

Let's start by unraveling the mystery of stress and its profound impact on the aging process. Stress is a physiological and psychological phenomenon that nudges the course of our health and well-being, rather than a feeling that disappears quickly.

Physiologically, our bodies respond to stress through a cascade of reactions, activating the famed "fight or flight" response that gears us up to face imminent threats. Cue the release of hormones like cortisol and adrenaline, our body's superheroes in dealing with immediate threats. These stress hormones were once our trusty allies, designed to help us sprint away from predators. But in our modern jungle of deadlines and worries, they can overstay their welcome.

Now, let's talk about these hormones. Cortisol, our body's natural alarm system, can be a bit overzealous. It's like a fire alarm that keeps ringing even after the toaster incident has been sorted.

But here's the twist: While this response is vital for survival in short bursts, prolonged or chronic stress can take a toll on our bodies as the years roll by. Our cells, those minuscule powerhouses of life, bear the brunt of this chronic stress. Telomeres, the protective caps at the ends of our chromosomes, are like the ticking clock of our cellular aging process. Think of it this way: Our body's stress response is like a fire alarm. It's meant to ring out in emergencies, but if it's on all the time— well, that's a problem. Constant stress can lead to inflammation, compromising our immune system, and even accelerating the aging process at a cellular level.

Let's zoom into the psychological dance between stress and aging. Our minds are powerful players in this game. The way we perceive stress, how we cope with it, and the resilience we cultivate all shape the impact it has on our aging journey.

Reducing stress isn't just about keeping our cool—it's a ticket to the fountain of youth. Studies have whispered a secret that ancient yogis and wise elders have known all along: Stress reduction can be a gateway to a longer, healthier life. When we ease the grip of stress, we might as well be handing ourselves the elixir of longevity.

Stress-Reduction Techniques: Unlocking the Elixir of Longevity

Now that we've uncovered the relationship between stress and aging, let's equip ourselves with an arsenal of stress-busting techniques. Think of these strategies as your personalized keys to the fountain of youth, each crafted to suit different lifestyles and preferences.

Breathing Exercises for Immediate Stress Relief

Have you ever caught yourself in the act of mouth-breathing or found your chest feeling like it's hosting a traffic jam instead of your belly? That's our body's way of signaling dysfunction in our breathing patterns. It's like playing a song on repeat but missing the melody.

Here's where we need to return to the roots, to what I like to call "belly breathing," or diaphragmatic breathing. Picture how a baby effortlessly breathes, their tiny belly rising and falling like a gentle wave. That's the sweet spot we're aiming for. Become your own breath detective. Mind the moments when your breathing turns dysfunctional. Is it during a tense meeting? When facing a looming deadline? By recognizing these patterns, you're taking a proactive step toward managing stress. It's like catching a storm on the horizon before it reaches the shore.

Belly breathing is a powerful stress antidote, instantly calming the storm within. An important note: It should always be nose breathing; our nose plays an important role for the air in our lungs.

As a calming and balancing exercise try the 5-5 technique: Inhale for a count of five and exhale for five, for three to five minutes. It's a simple but effective breath of fresh air for your body and mind and has shown to regenerate the nervous system, even hours later. If the 5-5 cycle is too difficult, try a 4-4, or even a 3-3. Sometimes stress is so exhausting that we feel breathless. Give yourself a go and try to make the next number every 5th breath. You can smoothly move your arms up to the ceiling while inhaling and down to the floor while exhaling; it intensifies the effect a little bit. This is also a good recovery technique after a workout.

Progressive Muscle Relaxation Techniques

Stress often occurs in our muscles, turning them into tense soldiers on high alert. Progressive muscle relaxation is your secret weapon against this tension. Start by tensing and then slowly releasing each muscle group, from head to toe. It's like giving your body a massage from the inside, a soothing reset button for your stressed-out muscles.

Visualization and Guided Imagery for Mental Calmness

Our minds are powerful architects of reality. Visualization and guided imagery are tools that let you design a mental sanctuary where stress isn't invited. Picture yourself in a serene place—maybe a beach at sunset or a quiet mountain cabin. Engage your senses, feel the warmth of the sun or the cool mountain breeze. It's not just daydreaming; it's creating a mental safe haven.

Sit or lie down and focus on your belly-breathing. Relax your body while exhaling and breathe at a comfortable pace. Create a safe and beloved place in your imagination. Stay there and savor that feeling for a while. Customize the surroundings to your liking. Choose an object within your imaginary sight and make it soar into the sky. Observe it for some time. This object now symbolizes being in good hands and feeling relaxed, knowing that nothing can harm you. The next time you feel stressed, visualize this symbol in your mind's eye and see what happens.

Lifestyle Modifications for Long-Term Stress Reduction

Sometimes, the key to stress reduction lies in tweaking our daily habits. It's not about a radical overhaul but small, sustainable changes that accumulate into a fortress against stress. Prioritize sleep, nurture your body with nutritious food, and embrace physical activity. A well-nourished, well-rested body is better equipped to handle the curveballs life throws.

Never count out the importance of having fun! Fun is best in really stressful situations, and it is highly underestimated in life, generally. Recent studies show remarkable results in incorporating fun as a stress reducer and health supporter.

Now that we have a stress-busting toolkit at our disposal, it's time to integrate those techniques into our daily lives. Remember, stress reduction isn't a one-size-fits-all journey; it's about finding what resonates with you.

Start with small steps. Dedicate a few minutes each day to deep breathing or progressive muscle relaxation and have fun. Experiment with visualization and find the mental landscapes that speak to your soul. Gradually incorporate lifestyle modifications, making them a natural part of your routine rather than an overwhelming upheaval.

Holistic Approaches to Stress Reduction

Now that we've laid the foundation with fundamental stress-reduction techniques, let's venture into the world of holistic approaches. Picture them as the extra spices in your stress-busting recipe, enhancing the flavor of your journey toward holistic well-being.

The Science Behind Alternative Therapies

Acupuncture, aromatherapy, and massage may seem like luxuries, but their impact on stress is backed by science. Acupuncture, an ancient Chinese practice, involves inserting thin needles into specific points to rebalance the body's energy flow. It's not just about the needles but about where those needles are placed, unlocking the flow of calmness within.

Aromatherapy, with its fragrant oils and soothing scents, taps into the powerful connection between smell and emotion. Essential oils like lavender and chamomile can transform your space into a haven of tranquility, signaling to your mind that it's time to unwind.

And who can forget the magic of a good massage? Beyond its feel-good factor, massage can reduce cortisol levels and increase the release of endorphins, your body's natural stress fighters. It's like giving your muscles a vacation while your mind takes a break.

Integrating Holistic Therapies Into Daily Life

Now, let's talk about practicality. These therapies aren't reserved for spa days; they can become integral parts of your daily routine. Consider scheduling a monthly acupuncture session, infusing your living space with calming scents, or even incorporating self-massage into your bedtime routine.

You don't need to overhaul your life, but infusing it with moments of peace and relaxation can help reduce stress, which benefits you overall. Imagine coming home to the subtle aroma of lavender, dimming the lights, and treating yourself to a brief massage. Suddenly, stress takes a backseat, and your home becomes a sanctuary.

Finding Your Holistic Harmony

In the grand symphony of stress reduction, holistic approaches are the intricate melodies that harmonize through the basics. They're not reserved for the elite; they're accessible notes that anyone can integrate into their daily lives. So, as you embark on this journey, consider these holistic approaches as the extra instruments in your orchestra of well-being. Each session of acupuncture, every whiff of calming essential oil, and every gentle massage is a stroke on the canvas of your stress-free masterpiece.

Mindfulness and Aging: A Fountain of Youth for the Mind

As we navigate the journey of aging, the practice of mindfulness emerges as a timeless ally, offering not just a respite but a meaningful transformation for the mind. Let's unravel the treasure trove of benefits reaped by mindfulness and meditation, exploring their intricate role in fostering mental wellness and graceful aging.

Benefits of Mindfulness: Beyond the Surface

Mindfulness is a transformative tool. At its core, mindfulness is about being present, embracing each moment without judgment. Research has showcased its profound impact on mental wellness, especially with stress reduction. As we age, stress can become an unwelcome companion, but mindfulness offers a way to bid it adieu.

Mindfulness can be a soothing balm that eases the tension in both the mind and body. The practice of mindfulness redirects our focus from the whirlwind of worries to the present moment, where the richness of life unfolds.

As cortisol levels lower, the body's inflammatory responses ease, contributing to a healthier aging process. It's not about eliminating stress entirely—that's a mythical quest. Instead, it's about changing our relationship with stress, ensuring it doesn't overshadow the grace of growing older.

Improving Emotional Regulation Through Mindfulness

Emotions, the colorful threads in the fabric of our existence, can sometimes become entangled. Mindfulness is the untangling process, fostering emotional regulation that is essential for mental well-being. By observing our thoughts and feelings without judgment, we cultivate a space for understanding and acceptance.

Mindfulness is about understanding emotions rather than suppressing them, allowing us to respond thoughtfully rather than react impulsively. As we age, this emotional resilience becomes a treasure, enriching our relationships and deepening our connection with the world.

Now, how do we invite mindfulness into our lives? Most of us can't go sit on a mountaintop in perpetual meditation. But everyone can infuse mindfulness into the rhythm of our daily activities. Whether it's savoring the taste of a cup of tea, having fun, feeling the warmth of the sun on our skin, or simply being fully present with our thoughts, each moment becomes an opportunity for mindfulness.

Consider integrating short meditation sessions into your routine, embracing mindful walking, or engaging in activities that bring you joy. It's not a rigid practice; it's a fluid dance with the present moment, inviting a sense of calmness into your daily life.

Mindful Practices for Mental Health

So, you've decided to embark on the journey of mindfulness as a living, breathing part of your everyday life rather than a distant concept. Let's look at practical and accessible mindful practices that transform ordinary moments into opportunities for mental nourishment.

Mindful Breathing Exercises for Stress Alleviation

Let's begin with an anchor that's always with you: your breath. Mindful breathing exercises are like minivacations for your mind. Try this simple yet powerful technique: Close your eyes, take a deep breath in through your nose, feel the air filling your lungs, and then exhale slowly through your mouth. Repeat this several times, allowing your breath to become a gentle rhythm by exhaling the lips, which should press the air a bit.

Then go on to a 7-minute meditation with normal nostril- and belly-breathing; try to focus only on your breath. Sooner or later your mind gets bored and comes up with distracting thoughts–that is completely normal! As soon as you detect these thoughts, accept them, send them away on an imaginary cloud, and focus on your breath again. Set a timer for 7 minutes. The more you practice this, the more full your mind will get

In moments of stress or overwhelm, pause and take a few mindful breaths. In doing so, you can ground yourself in the present, giving your mind a moment of reprieve.

Mindfulness-Based Stress Reduction (MBSR) Techniques

Mindfulness-Based Stress Reduction (MBSR) is a structured program designed to integrate mindfulness into daily life. Don't worry; you don't need a manual. Start with a body scan—a simple practice wherein you bring attention to different parts of your body, releasing tension as you go. It's a bit like giving your body a mindful massage from the inside.

Another technique involves mindful walking. Instead of rushing from point A to point B, savor each step. Feel the earth beneath your feet, notice the subtle movements of your body, and let the world unfold around you. It's not a race, but a journey of awareness.

Mindful Eating for Improved Mental Well-being

Eating isn't just about fueling the body; it's an opportunity for mindfulness. Engage in mindful eating by paying attention to each bite. Notice the textures, flavors, and sensations. Put away distractions—no scrolling through your phone or catching up on emails. It's a date with your food.

Try this: Before you start your meal, take a moment to appreciate its colors and aromas. Chew slowly, savoring each mouthful. Not only does this enhance your connection with your food, it promotes a sense of satisfaction and gratitude.

Incorporating mindfulness into your life is an ongoing practice. Consider setting aside a few minutes each day for a mindfulness ritual. It could be a morning breathing exercise, a lunchtime mindful walk, or an evening reflection.

Make it your own. Feel free to explore and mix these practices, adapting them to your preferences and schedule. The goal isn't perfection; it's the sincere effort to bring mindfulness into your life, transforming routine activities into moments of reflection and presence.

Mindfulness and the Aging Brain

As we continue to discover the benefits of mindfulness, let's explore its remarkable impact on the aging brain. The connection between mindfulness and our brain's health is more than just a passing acquaintance; it's a transformative relationship that can shape the course of our cognitive well-being.

Enter the world of neuroplasticity—the brain's marvelous ability to rewire and adapt. Mindfulness is more than just a fleeting thought; it's a catalyst for change within the intricate networks of our brain. Through practices like meditation and mindfulness exercises, we stimulate this neuroplasticity, sculpting the brain's structure and function.

Imagine it as a mental workout—each moment of mindful presence flexes the brain's muscles, strengthening neural connections and nurturing cognitive resilience. This isn't wishful thinking; it's science illuminating the path toward a vibrant brain.

Aging is more than just the passage of time; it's about preserving the essence of who we are. Mindfulness emerges as a shield against cognitive decline, offering a toolkit to fortify the mind's resilience. Studies have whispered tales of its prowess—how mindfulness practices can mitigate the effects of aging on the brain.

By engaging in regular mindfulness exercises, we foster cognitive agility, enhancing attention, memory, and executive functions. During the process, we're embracing aging with a mind that remains sharp, curious, and adaptable.

So, how do we make mindfulness a cornerstone of brain health? Start by acknowledging the power of consistency. A daily dose of mindfulness isn't just a routine; it's an investment in your brain's well-being. Consider dedicating specific moments to mindfulness exercises, be it a morning meditation, midday mental pause, or an evening reflection.

Explore different techniques that resonate with you. Whether it's focused attention meditation or loving-kindness practices, find the ones that feel like a mental embrace. Remember, it's not about striving for perfection; it's about the earnest effort to nourish your brain with moments of mindful presence.

Cognitive Health and Age-Related Decline

Now that we understand the symbiotic relationship between mindfulness and the aging brain, let's expand our toolkit to include a variety of techniques specifically designed to maintain cognitive abilities. Think of these as daily exercises that flex the muscles of your mind, ensuring they remain nimble and resilient.

Techniques to Maintain Cognitive Abilities

Brain-Training Exercises and Cognitive Games

Consider this the gym for your brain—a place where mental muscles are challenged and strengthened. Engage in brain-training exercises and cognitive games designed to stimulate various cognitive functions. Puzzle games, crosswords, and Sudoku are like calisthenics for your brain, keeping it agile and ready for the intellectual dance of life.

In the digital age, numerous apps and online platforms offer a plethora of brain-training games. From memory exercises to pattern-recognition challenges, these activities are both enjoyable and effective in maintaining cognitive abilities. And sure, winning is fun, but so is the journey of mental exploration.

Learning New Skills to Stimulate the Brain

Your brain thrives on novelty. Learning new skills is akin to giving your brain a fresh playground to explore. Whether it's picking up a musical instrument, learning a new language, or mastering a craft, each new skill activates different neural networks.

The process of learning is a dance between challenge and reward. It encourages the brain to create new connections and pathways, fostering cognitive flexibility. So, embrace the excitement of being a perpetual learner—your brain will thank you for it.

Social Engagement and Its Impact on Cognitive Health

Humans are inherently social beings—our brains revel in the company of others. Social engagement is more than just a pleasant pastime; it's a powerful elixir for cognitive health. Interacting with friends, family, and the community stimulates various cognitive functions.

Engage in conversations that require active listening and thoughtful responses. Join clubs, attend social events, or volunteer for community activities. The shared experiences and diverse perspectives encountered in social interactions contribute to the cognitive richness of your brain. Consider dedicating a portion of your day to brain-training games, alternating between different activities to keep things fresh and engaging. Have fun while exercising your mind.

As you learn new skills, embrace the joy of discovery and the sense of accomplishment that comes with mastering something new. Incorporate social engagements into your routine, creating opportunities for shared experiences that will brighten your day as well as enrich your cognitive landscape.

Preventing Age-Related Cognitive Decline: Embracing Lifestyle Choices

Let's take a deeper look at the role lifestyle choices play in the grand symphony of preventing or delaying cognitive decline. Your lifestyle isn't just a series of routines; it's a conductor orchestrating the harmony of your cognitive health. Join me as we explore the keys to this symphony.

The Impact of Diet and Nutrition on Cognitive Health

Consider your diet as brain fuel. Just as a car needs quality fuel to run efficiently, your brain thrives on nourishing foods. Embrace a diet rich in antioxidants, omega-3 fatty acids, and vitamins. Think colorful fruits and vegetables, nuts, and seeds.

These nutrients act as brain defenders, reducing oxidative stress and inflammation, which are detrimental to cognitive health. So, indulge in a brain-boosting meal that not only satiates your taste buds but also nurtures your cognitive garden.

Sleep Quality and Its Influence on Cognitive Abilities

When it comes to cognitive health, sleep is your brain's recharge station. Quality sleep isn't a luxury; it's a necessity for cognitive function. During sleep, your brain undergoes a cleaning process, removing toxins that accumulate during the day. This restoration is essential for cognitive functions like learning, problem-solving, and decision-making. So, prioritize sleep as an investment in your brain's longevity.

Prioritize sleep hygiene—create a calming bedtime routine, limit screen time before sleep, and ensure your sleep environment is conducive to rest. As with so many things in life, it's about quality, not just quantity. Good-quality sleep rejuvenates your mind and fortifies its cognitive reserves.

Studies say that only 1 out of 100,000 people can get away with fewer than 7 hours of sleep. So the chances that you need more than 7 hours are very high—and very underestimated. Make sure you get 7–9 hours every night. Studies also show that you cannot sleep more one night to compensate for a different night of less sleep—you can improve cognitive ability during the day with naps, but you cannot make up for fewer than 7 hours of good rest.

Studies also show that you lose the recovery of the brain (a very healthy part of it) by not sleeping enough. Naps don't help; they are very good for cognitive recovery and an excellent rejuvenate strategy, however.

Physical Exercise and Its Cognitive Benefits

Exercise isn't just a gift for your body; it's a feast for your brain. Engaging in regular physical activity enhances blood flow to the brain, promoting the growth of new brain cells and fostering neuroplasticity. It's like aerobics for your mind.

Aim for a mix of activities—whether it's brisk walking, dancing, yoga, or even gardening. These exercises not only keep your body nimble but also sharpen your cognitive sword. The key isn't intensity; it's consistency. So, lace up those shoes and let your brain rejoice in the symphony of movement.

While incorporating these lifestyle changes into your daily life, make small, sustainable changes that eventually become your lifestyle companions.

A colorful plate of nutritious food, a restful night's sleep, and a joyful session of physical activity—these actions and movements are investments in your cognitive wealth. Embrace them not as chores but as pillars supporting the temple of your cognitive health and also a good amount of fun.

Lifelong Learning and Cognitive Agility: Unfolding the Mind's Tapestry

Let's keep exploring the art of preserving cognitive function through the perpetual dance of learning and intellectual engagement. Your mind isn't a stagnant pond; it's an ever-flowing river, and lifelong learning is the current that keeps it vibrant and agile. Join me as we explore the canvas of your mind's potential.

Exploring Hobbies and Activities that Stimulate the Mind

Hobbies are more than just pastimes; they're invitations for your mind to wander through uncharted territories. Whether it's diving into the world of literature, mastering a new craft, or exploring the mysteries of science, each hobby is a brushstroke painting the canvas of your cognitive landscape.

Consider hobbies that challenge and stimulate your mind. Puzzle-solving, playing musical instruments, gardening, or even engaging in strategic games—these all contribute to mental gymnastics. Choose activities that ignite your passion and curiosity, keeping your mind in a perpetual state of exploration.

The Importance of Staying Curious and Open-Minded

Curiosity is the spark that ignites the flame of learning. Cultivate a curious mind, one that thrives on questions rather than answers. As the saying goes, curiosity didn't kill the cat; it made it a lifelong learner. Stay open-minded, welcoming new ideas and perspectives like a sponge soaking in the richness of knowledge.

Challenge your assumptions, seek diverse viewpoints, attend lectures, join book clubs, or participate in discussions that challenge your viewpoints. The mind that remains open is the mind that continues to evolve, adapting to the changing landscapes of knowledge and wisdom.

Incorporating these practices isn't about adding items to your to-do list; it's about embracing the joy of exploration. It's not about forcing yourself to learn; it's about finding delight in the process of discovery.

Make learning a daily ritual, a new, exciting part of your life. Read books that pique your curiosity, engage in discussions that challenge your perspectives, and explore new territories with the hunger of a lifelong learner.

Lifelong learning is about the joy of discovery, the thrill of understanding, and the empowerment of knowledge. It's a perpetual flame that illuminates the corridors of your mind, warding off the shadows of cognitive decline.

Consider enrolling in classes, whether in person or online, that ignite your passion or introduce you to new subjects. Embrace the adventure of continuous learning, where each lesson is a stepping stone in the grand mosaic of your intellectual growth.

Your mind is a garden that flourishes when tended to with the waters of knowledge. So, read that book, learn that instrument, and explore the realms of understanding that beckon you. As you embark on this journey of lifelong learning, let each discovery be a testament to the eternal flame of your cognitive vitality.

Biohacking the Mind for Enhanced Well-Being: Embracing Technology's Role

In our ever-evolving world, technology has become so much more than just a tool; it's a bridge to nurturing mental well-being, especially as we gracefully age. Let's explore the intersection where technology meets the mind, offering innovative interventions to enhance our mental vitality.

In our tech-driven era, innovation is not just confined to the external; it extends to the inner landscapes of our minds. Explore the fascinating world where technology and mental wellness converge, offering tools and insights to enhance the quality of your cognitive life.

Wearable Devices for Stress Tracking and Management

As we mentioned in Chapters 1 and 3, you can have a personal assistant—not on your desk, but on your wrist. Meet the world of wearable devices designed to track and manage stress. These devices monitor physiological indicators like heart-rate variability, providing real-time feedback on your stress levels.

Explore devices like Fitbit, Apple Watch, or Garmin, which provide data on your stress levels throughout the day. The key is not just to collect data but to use it as a compass, guiding you toward activities and practices that soothe the mind.

Consider integrating a stress-tracking wearable into your routine, which can help you raise awareness of what's going on with your body. Recognizing patterns in your stress response empowers you to make informed lifestyle choices, ensuring that your cognitive garden remains resilient in the face of daily challenges.

Brainwave Entrainment Technology for Relaxation and Focus Enhancement

Ever heard of brainwave entrainment? It's like a symphony conductor guiding your brain waves to specific frequencies for relaxation or focus. Technology offers auditory or visual stimuli that synchronize brain activity, inducing states of calmness or sharpened focus.

Whether you're seeking relaxation or a mental boost, these technologies offer tailored experiences. These tools act as companions in your quest for mental balance, offering a digital ally in your pursuit of cognitive well-being.

Explore Apps and Devices

- **Binaural beats apps:** These apps use stereo sound to create a perceived third frequency, influencing brainwave patterns for relaxation or focus.

- **Light-and-sound machines:** Devices like the Lucia N°03 use light and sound to induce altered states of consciousness, promoting relaxation and mental clarity.

- **Mindfulness apps with guided meditations:** Apps like Headspace and Calm incorporate technology to deliver guided meditation sessions with calming sounds and visuals.

These tools can make great companions on your journey toward a balanced and focused mind.

Apps and Digital Platforms Promoting Mental Health

Your smartphone is more than a communication device; it's a gateway to mental wellness. Explore a plethora of apps and digital platforms designed to support your mental health journey. From guided-meditation apps to mood-tracking platforms, these tools offer personalized interventions at your fingertips.

Consider incorporating mental health apps into your daily routine. Whether it's a mindfulness app for a quick meditation session or a journaling app for reflection, let your device be a digital sanctuary supporting your cognitive flourishing.

Some Noteworthy Mental Health Apps

- **Headspace:** Known for guided meditation and mindfulness exercises.

- **Calm:** Offers guided meditations, sleep stories, and relaxation techniques.

- **Lumosity:** Focuses on brain-training games to enhance cognitive abilities.

- **Moodpath:** A mood-tracking app that helps you understand and manage your emotions.

- **Wysa:** An AI chatbot designed to provide emotional support and coping strategies.

Incorporating these technological interventions and embracing tools that amplify our mental well-being can create companions supporting your journey toward mental vitality.

Explore these technologies with curiosity, but also discernment. They are tools, and how you wield them matters. Use them as aids on your path to mental well-being, allowing them to complement your lifestyle choices and holistic practices.

As we learn and discover more about mental wellness, we can go on a personalized journey—a biohacking adventure tailored to your individual needs. Just as our fingerprints are unique, so are the keys to unlocking your mental vitality. Let's explore biohacking approaches that cater to your distinct mental landscape.

Brain Stimulation Methods for Mood Regulation

Step into the world of brain stimulation, where subtle interventions can influence your mood and cognitive state. Transcranial magnetic stimulation (TMS) and transcranial direct current stimulation (tDCS) are examples of techniques that gently modulate brain activity.

These noninvasive methods offer personalized interventions, fine-tuning brain circuits to enhance mood or alleviate symptoms of depression. They're not just about tweaking neural networks but about crafting personalized melodies for your mental harmony.

Nutritional Supplements and Nootropics for Cognitive Enhancement

Explore the palette of nutritional supplements and nootropics—substances believed to enhance cognitive function. Omega-3 fatty acids, vitamin B-complex, and adaptogens like rhodiola rosea are among the natural compounds that might contribute to cognitive well-being.

They're not magic pills; they're companions in your quest for cognitive enhancement. When combined with a balanced diet, they can serve as personalized nutrients that fuel your brain's vitality.

However, tread cautiously in this realm. Consult with healthcare professionals or nutritionists to determine the right supplements suited for your individual needs and health conditions. The goal is not just enhancement; it's optimization in alignment with your holistic well-being.

Personalized mental wellness isn't about adopting a one-size-fits-all approach–nothing in this book is–but, rather, about crafting your unique symphony. Biohacking is an art, and you are the artist. Explore these techniques with a discerning eye, listen to your body's cues, and fine-tune the interventions that resonate with your unique composition.

It's an ongoing journey of self-discovery. Your body communicates its needs, and these biohacking approaches are tools in your hands. Use them with intention, curiosity, and an awareness that your mental wellness is a canvas waiting for your personal strokes.

Ethical Considerations and Future Trends

As we navigate the ever-evolving landscape of mental-wellness biohacking, it's essential to consider the ethical implications of our choices and peek into the future to anticipate the trends that might shape the path ahead.

Privacy Concerns When Using Mental Health Apps and Devices

In the era of data-driven insights, privacy becomes a paramount concern. As we entrust our mental health to technology, questions arise about how our sensitive data is handled. Mental-health apps and devices often collect intimate information about our emotions, stress levels, and daily habits.

Consider opting for platforms with robust privacy policies that prioritize the confidentiality of your data. Scrutinize the terms of use, understand data-collection practices, and seek transparency from these platforms. Be mindful of the permissions you grant, and stay informed about how your information is utilized. In the quest for mental wellness, ensure that the journey doesn't compromise the sanctuary of your personal information.

Advancements in Neurotechnology and Their Potential Impact on Mental Well-Being

Fasten your seatbelts as we embark on a journey into the future—one in which neurotechnology could reshape the landscape of mental well-being. Advances in neurofeedback, brain-machine interfaces, and neurostimulation hold promises and pose challenges. As advancements continue, the potential impact on our well-being is vast and multifaceted. Imagine neurofeedback technologies becoming more accessible, enabling individuals to modulate brain activity for emotional regulation or cognitive enhancement.

While this holds tremendous potential, it also raises ethical questions about consent, potential misuse, and the delicate balance between augmentation and preservation of natural cognitive functions. Anticipate ethical debates surrounding neuroenhancement and the ethical boundaries of altering brain function. Uphold values that prioritize ethical usage, ensuring these technologies are harnessed for the betterment of mental health without unforeseen consequences.

As biohacking enthusiasts, we stand at the crossroads of ethics and innovation. It's okay to push boundaries, but it must be done ethically. Engage with technology but hold it accountable. Advocate for transparency in how technology companies handle mental health data. Champion platforms that prioritize user privacy and consent, and advocate for responsible innovation in the neurotechnology landscape.

The journey ahead is not just a technological expedition; it's a moral compass guiding us toward a future where mental wellness and ethical considerations walk hand in hand. Let your choices, your advocacy, and your engagement with these technologies echo your values.

Chapter 5:

Chronic Condition Management

Aging gracefully often comes with a few companions—health conditions that seem to tap on our shoulders as the years go by. These guests, though unwelcome, are not uncommon. Conditions like arthritis, cardiovascular diseases, osteoporosis, and a host of others tend to show up more frequently as we journey through life.

Arthritis, for instance, can be like an uninvited guest, making its presence known through joint pain and stiffness. Cardiovascular diseases, the silent assailants, can challenge our heart's rhythm and function. Osteoporosis, the quiet underminer, can weaken our bones, making a simple tumble a more concerning event.

These conditions aren't just names on a medical chart; they're intruders that can disrupt our daily rhythms and affect our overall well-being. Picture this: waking up with stiff joints that make every step feel like a negotiation with discomfort or feeling the weight of fatigue from a heart that's working overtime. These conditions can color our days with challenges that test our patience and resilience.

But let's not paint a bleak picture here. Despite their disruptive tendencies, managing these conditions is not a lost cause. The key lies in understanding, support, and a dose of optimism.

As we navigate the realm of managing age-related conditions, it's crucial to understand that aging can add a layer of complexity to the equation. Imagine dealing with arthritis in your 30s versus your 70s—the experience and challenges can vary significantly. Let's explore the unique considerations that come into play as we age, shedding light on how these factors contribute to the landscape of age-related conditions.

Factors Contributing to Age-Related Conditions

- **Biological changes:** More than just a number, aging is a process that affects our bodies at a cellular level. Our joints may show signs of wear and tear, and our cardiovascular system might face changes in elasticity and efficiency. These biological shifts can contribute to conditions like arthritis and cardiovascular diseases.

- **Decreased resilience:** Picture our bodies as superheroes, equipped with an incredible ability to heal and recover. However, as we age, our superhero capes may not flutter as vigorously. The body's ability to bounce back from stressors may diminish, making it essential to adopt a proactive approach to health.

- **Cumulative lifestyle effects:** The choices we make throughout our lives play a significant role in shaping our health. A lifetime of habits, both positive and negative, can accumulate and manifest in various conditions. For instance, a history of sedentary behavior may contribute to the development of osteoporosis, emphasizing the importance of lifelong health-conscious decisions.

- **Genetic predispositions:** Our genetic makeup can influence our susceptibility to certain conditions. While we can't rewrite our genetic code, understanding our family's health history empowers us to take preventive measures and manage potential risks more effectively.

- **Nutritional needs and absorption:** Aging can impact our body's ability to absorb nutrients, potentially leading to deficiencies. Adequate nutrition becomes a crucial component in managing and preventing age-related conditions. The importance of eating right to nourish our bodies through the years cannot be understated.

Despite these age-specific considerations, it's essential to emphasize that proactive management is within our grasp. The wisdom of age grants us the insight to make informed choices, the patience to adapt, and the resilience to face challenges head-on.

In-Depth Exploration of Chronic Conditions

Cardiovascular Health

Cardiovascular health is a vital aspect of our well-being, especially as we age. Understanding the complexities of cardiovascular diseases and their risk factors is the first step toward effective management.

Picture the heart as the engine of our body, tirelessly pumping life throughout. But like any engine, it requires care and maintenance. Factors like high blood pressure, cholesterol levels, diabetes, and lifestyle choices contribute significantly to cardiovascular health. However, managing these factors involves a combination of lifestyle modifications and, in some cases, medical interventions.

Lifestyle Modifications

Let's talk lifestyle—a term often thrown around but profoundly impactful. Small changes in our daily habits can yield monumental effects on our cardiovascular well-being. From adopting heart-healthy diets rich in vegetables, fruits, and organic proteins (in this order) to embracing regular exercise routines, these modifications act as shields, fortifying our heart against potential risks.

Medical Interventions

In cases where lifestyle adjustments aren't sufficient, medical interventions step in as invaluable tools. Medications to regulate blood pressure or cholesterol levels, surgical procedures to restore blood flow, and innovative therapies serve as pillars in managing cardiovascular conditions.

Osteoarthritis and Joint Health

Now, let's shift our focus to a common companion of aging: joint issues, with osteoarthritis taking center stage. These conditions can turn the simple act of movement into a challenge, but they need not confine us to a life of discomfort.

Osteoarthritis, often characterized by the breakdown of cartilage in joints, is a leading cause of chronic joint pain in aging populations. However, understanding its triggers and manifestations equips us with the tools to manage and mitigate its impact.

Exercise Routines

The notion of exercising while dealing with joint pain might seem contradictory, but it's a crucial piece of the puzzle. Tailored exercise routines, incorporating low-impact activities like swimming or cycling, can strengthen muscles surrounding the joints, providing support and reducing pain.

Pain-Management Strategies

Beyond exercise, a repertoire of pain-management strategies becomes essential. From heat and cold therapies to the use of assistive devices and, when needed, medications, these approaches offer relief and enable individuals to reclaim a more active and comfortable lifestyle.

Some operations can help if there is too much damage to a joint. My mother had to go to three doctors to find one that would operate on her knee—they said she was too old! She healed quickly, unlike the first two doctors' predictions, and her knee is now pain free. She can ski again and walk everywhere, which gives her a huge confidence booster. As I mentioned in the beginning of the book, she went through a rough time; once she felt healthier, in less pain, her emotional health improved as well.

Metabolic Health

As we age, our metabolism can undergo changes, impacting how our bodies process and utilize energy. Understanding these shifts and employing strategies to maintain metabolic health becomes pivotal in our journey toward healthy aging.

Picture metabolism as the body's engine, converting what we eat and drink into energy. With age, this engine may start to sputter a bit, slowing down the rate at which we burn calories. Muscle mass diminishes, affecting our basal metabolic rate. Hormonal changes and decreased physical activity can further influence our metabolic functions. Understanding these changes allows us to adopt strategies that cater to our evolving metabolic needs.

Nutrition for Metabolic Well-Being

Fueling our bodies with the right nutrients becomes increasingly vital as we age. Nutrition isn't just about eating; it's about fueling our bodies with the right ingredients. A diet rich in fiber, organic proteins, and whole grains help regulate blood-sugar levels and maintain a healthy weight as well as support metabolic function. It's not about restrictive measures but about making informed and sustainable choices that nourish our bodies from the inside out.

Exercise for Metabolic Health

The symbiotic relationship between exercise and metabolism is a powerful one. Physical activity not only burns calories but also enhances insulin sensitivity, a key player in metabolic health. From brisk walks to strength training, finding activities that align with our preferences and abilities contributes to a metabolically resilient lifestyle.

Neurological Conditions

Age-related neurological conditions, such as dementia and Alzheimer's disease, often raise concern due to their impact on cognitive function. Understanding these conditions and the lifestyle factors that can influence their development becomes crucial in navigating this aspect of healthy aging. According to the latest science, these conditions also have a lot to do with metabolic health, and our metabolic health is closely related to food, movement, and sleep habits. Current studies are discovering how much we can gain back with training our brains using memory and thinking games. But until there is more data, it is not a bad habit to implement in our lives.

Understanding Dementia and Alzheimer's

Dementia encompasses a range of conditions affecting cognitive abilities, memory, and reasoning. Alzheimer's disease, the most common form of dementia, progressively impairs memory and thinking skills. While these conditions can be daunting, proactive measures can influence their onset and progression.

Mitigating Risks Through Lifestyle Factors

Research suggests that certain lifestyle choices can potentially reduce the risk of developing dementia or Alzheimer's disease. These factors include staying mentally active through continued learning, engaging in social activities to stimulate the mind, adopting a balanced diet rich in antioxidants and omega-3 fatty acids, and maintaining physical activity.

Cognitive Exercises and Brain Health Strategies

Just as physical exercise strengthens the body, cognitive exercises play a pivotal role in maintaining brain health. Activities that challenge the mind, such as puzzles, reading, learning new skills or languages, and engaging in stimulating conversations, act as a workout for the brain, promoting cognitive resilience.

Beyond specific exercises, maintaining overall health is paramount. Adequate sleep, stress-management techniques, and regular health check-ups contribute to a holistic approach to brain health.

Medication Alternatives

When it comes to managing chronic conditions, the conventional path often involves medications to alleviate symptoms or slow disease progression. However, the landscape of health and wellness is vast, offering a spectrum of alternative approaches that can complement or, in some cases, replace traditional medications. Let's explore these holistic alternatives that promote well-being from a more comprehensive standpoint.

Holistic Approaches to Chronic Condition Management

Imagine a toolkit filled not only with prescription bottles but also with nature's remedies and lifestyle adjustments. Holistic approaches embrace the interconnectedness of body, mind, and spirit, recognizing that true well-being extends beyond symptom management.

Dietary Supplements and Herbal Interventions

Nature has provided an array of supplements and herbs that can play a role in managing chronic conditions. From omega-3 fatty acids for cardiovascular health to turmeric's anti-inflammatory properties, these natural interventions can complement traditional treatments. Psyllium husks are a top fiber source that aids digestion, and glucosamin works well for cartilage lubrication. It's essential to approach dietary supplements with an informed perspective, consulting healthcare professionals to ensure compatibility with existing medications and individual health needs.

Mind-Body Therapies

The mind and body share an intricate dance, influencing each other in profound ways. Practices like acupuncture, meditation, and yoga harness this mind-body connection to promote healing and enhance overall well-being.

Acupuncture: An Ancient Art of Healing

Acupuncture, rooted in ancient Chinese medicine, involves the insertion of thin needles into specific points on the body to stimulate energy flow. Research suggests that acupuncture can offer relief for conditions such as chronic pain, arthritis, and even cardiovascular issues by promoting the body's natural healing mechanisms.

Meditation: Cultivating Mindful Awareness

The practice of meditation transcends its stereotype of mysticism, emerging as a scientifically supported method for managing stress, anxiety, and even chronic pain. Through mindfulness meditation, individuals can develop a heightened awareness of their thoughts and emotions, fostering a sense of calm and resilience in the face of health challenges.

Tai Chi and Pilates: Union of Body and Mind

Yoga, with its roots in ancient Indian philosophy, combines physical postures, breath control, and meditation. This holistic practice has demonstrated benefits in managing conditions such as arthritis, promoting flexibility, strength, and mental well-being.

Evidence-Based Mind-Body Interventions

While these mind-body therapies may sound like ancient wisdom, modern science continues to unveil the evidence supporting their efficacy. Rigorous research studies have demonstrated the tangible benefits of practices like acupuncture, Tai Chi, pilates, meditation, and yoga in reducing pain, improving mental health, and enhancing overall quality of life for individuals dealing with chronic conditions.

Personalized Medicine

As technology advances and our understanding of genetics deepens, the future of personalized medicine in chronic condition management holds immense promise. From targeted drug therapies to lifestyle recommendations customized for genetic predispositions, this approach heralds a new era in healthcare—one that prioritizes not just treating symptoms but understanding and addressing the root causes of individual health challenges.

The concept of personalized medicine marks a paradigm shift in healthcare—a move away from a one-size-fits-all approach to interventions tailored to individual health profiles. Recognizing that each person's body and health journey are unique, personalized medicine aims to optimize treatment plans based on genetic, environmental, and lifestyle factors.

Pain-Management Techniques

Where chronic conditions are concerned, pain often stands as a persistent companion, demanding attention and effective management strategies. While medications play a crucial role, exploring holistic approaches to pain management beyond pharmaceuticals offers a comprehensive toolkit to alleviate discomfort and enhance overall well-being. Let's look at nonpharmacological pain-management techniques, highlighting the role of physical therapy, rehabilitation, and psychological interventions in navigating the complexities of pain.

Nonpharmacological Pain Management

Physical Therapy and Rehabilitation: Rediscovering Movement

Physical therapy is more than just a regimen of exercises; it's a tailored approach to restoring and enhancing physical function. Whether grappling with joint pain, recovering from surgery, or managing the effects of chronic conditions, physical therapy plays a pivotal role in reacquainting individuals with the joy of movement.

Rehabilitation involves comprehensive programs designed to optimize recovery, combining physical therapy with lifestyle adjustments. It's not merely about addressing the symptoms but about fostering resilience, rebuilding strength, and reclaiming a sense of control over one's body.

Psychological Interventions for Pain: Nurturing the Mind-Body Connection

Pain is more than a physical phenomenon; it's intricately linked to our mental and emotional well-being. Psychological interventions provide valuable tools for managing pain by addressing the mind-body connection.

- **Cognitive-behavioral therapy (CBT):** CBT is a widely recognized approach that helps individuals reframe their thoughts and develop coping mechanisms. By changing how we perceive and respond to pain, CBT can significantly reduce its impact on daily life.

- **Mindfulness and relaxation techniques:** Practices such as mindfulness meditation and deep-breathing exercises bring attention to the present moment, helping individuals manage pain by promoting relaxation and reducing stress. These techniques empower individuals to navigate pain with a calm and centered mindset.

In exploring nonpharmacological pain management, the emphasis is on a comprehensive and personalized approach that recognizes the interconnectedness of the body and mind. These techniques offer not only relief from pain but also tools for empowerment, resilience, and an improved quality of life.

Physical Pain Management

When it comes to managing the physical aspects of pain associated with chronic conditions, a targeted approach tailored to specific discomforts becomes essential. Let's look into techniques aimed at addressing joint pain, muscle stiffness, and other physical discomforts, offering individuals a toolkit to alleviate these challenges and enhance their daily lives.

Addressing Joint Pain and Muscle Stiffness

For those grappling with joint pain, movement can feel like a negotiation with discomfort. Techniques such as gentle stretching exercises, hydrotherapy, and heat or cold therapy provide relief by easing muscle tension, improving flexibility, and reducing inflammation. For instance, targeted stretches for arthritis or tailored exercises under the guidance of a physical therapist can significantly alleviate joint discomfort.

Other techniques to address this includes:

- **Heat and cold therapies:** Applying heat or cold to affected areas can provide relief from joint pain and muscle stiffness. Warm compresses or heating pads relax muscles and increase blood flow, while cold packs can reduce inflammation and numb pain.

- **Massage and manual therapy:** Skilled hands can work wonders. Massage and manual-therapy techniques, whether performed by a professional or through self-massage, help alleviate tension, improve circulation, and promote flexibility.

- **Aquatic therapy:** Buoyancy in water reduces the impact on joints, making aquatic therapy an excellent option for managing pain associated with conditions like arthritis. The resistance of water also provides gentle strengthening exercises.

- **Gentle exercise and stretching:** Low-impact exercises, such as walking or tai chi, coupled with targeted stretches, can enhance flexibility and strength, promoting joint health and mitigating discomfort.

Muscle stiffness, often a companion of various conditions, can be managed through activities promoting relaxation and flexibility, such as yoga or tai chi. These practices not only improve physical comfort but also enhance overall well-being by incorporating mindfulness and breathing techniques.

Biohacking Solutions for Sleep and Pain

Tailoring interventions based on individual health profiles involves understanding genetic predispositions, lifestyle choices, and specific responses to treatments. This approach allows for more precise and effective strategies, reducing the risk of adverse reactions and optimizing positive outcomes.

Biohacking principles, focused on optimizing health and performance through personalized interventions, extend their reach beyond physical pain. They offer promising avenues for improving sleep quality, a vital component in managing pain and overall well-being.

Sleep hygiene encompasses practices that promote quality sleep. From maintaining a consistent sleep schedule to creating a comfortable sleep environment and practicing relaxation techniques before bedtime, these habits optimize the body's natural sleep-wake cycle.

Make sure the bedroom is dark (no lights from devices–best is to not have any devices in the bedroom), always go to bed at the same time and get up at the same time (with a 90-minute window), and if you take melatonin as a supplement, take it half-hour before sleep (though you should note that it doesn't improve your sleep so much as allow you to sleep in). Try different sleep times, and if you wear a sleep-tracking device, try to discern your natural sleep time (9–5, 10–6, 11–7, and so on). Your natural sleep time leaves you feeling most relaxed in the morning and falling asleep easily at night. Walking barefoot helps to regulate your system (there is actually evidence that supports this–it also helps with jet lag). Sunlight for 10 minutes first thing in the morning also helps as does taking a hot shower or a bath before sleep. (We need to cool down to sleep in, which is what a hot shower stimulates.) Finally, a mattress that helps regulate your temperature and good humidity and cold air in the bedroom will help you sleep as well.

Biohacking involves making small, intentional changes to optimize health and well-being. Applying biohacking principles to sleep may include using wearable devices to track sleep patterns; experimenting with sleep-inducing supplements or teas; and adjusting the timing and duration of sleep to align with natural circadian rhythms, ultimately influencing pain perception and overall health.

The Interconnectedness of Sleep, Pain, and Overall Health

The relationship between sleep and pain is intricate. Disrupted sleep can exacerbate pain sensitivity, while chronic pain can disrupt sleep patterns, creating a cyclical relationship. Understanding and addressing this interconnectedness becomes crucial in managing both pain and overall health.

Quality sleep not only provides a platform for the body to heal and repair but also regulates hormone levels, including those associated with pain perception. By optimizing sleep, individuals can potentially reduce pain intensity and improve their ability to cope with chronic conditions.

Sleep Optimization: Strategies for Better Sleep and Overall Health

Sleep, often dubbed the "ultimate biohack," plays a central role in overall health and well-being. Biohacking strategies aimed at optimizing sleep go beyond traditional sleep hygiene practices, incorporating technology and data-driven interventions.

Sleep-tracking devices, such as smart mattresses or wearable sleep trackers, provide detailed insights into sleep patterns. These devices monitor factors like sleep duration, sleep cycles, and disturbances, offering a comprehensive understanding of one's sleep quality.

Interventions based on this data may include personalized sleep schedules, personalized sleep-coaching apps, guided relaxation exercises, or even light and temperature adjustments to create an optimal sleep environment. By leveraging biohacking principles, individuals can tailor their approach to sleep, addressing specific factors that may be contributing to chronic conditions or exacerbating symptoms.

Chapter 6:

Retirement Planning—Embracing

a Purposeful Future

Retirement: that elusive yet eagerly anticipated phase of life when we hope to trade in the alarm clock for unhurried mornings and the 9-to-5 hustle for pursuits that truly light us up. It's a time when dreams deferred by work obligations might finally take center stage. But as we eagerly await this chapter of our lives, there's a fundamental groundwork that needs attention: our financial preparedness.

Let's face it: The prospect of retirement planning can feel as daunting as deciphering an ancient script. However, in this chapter, we are going to empower you to sail smoothly into the waters of retirement.

Financial wellness plays a pivotal role in determining the quality of our post-career years. When planning retirement, we want to ensure that what we've saved and accrued aligns with our aspirations, affording us the lifestyle we envision. So, where do we begin?

Financial wellness is the cornerstone of a fulfilling retirement. It's not just about counting dollars and cents; it's about feeling secure, confident, and ready for whatever life throws your way.

"Money can't buy happiness," they say, and they're right, but it sure can buy a sense of security and freedom. And isn't that a form of happiness in itself? Financial wellness means having the resources to live the life you desire, pursue your passions, and weather unexpected storms without losing sleep.

Assessing Financial Readiness for Retirement

Now, let's get real about where you stand financially. No judgment, just a friendly chat about making sure you're on the right track. Grab a notebook, if you want, or just let this information marinate in your mind.

- **Know your numbers:** Take stock of your current financial situation. What are your assets, debts, and monthly expenses? This isn't about scolding yourself for that impulse buy last month but understanding your financial landscape.

- **Create a budget:** Yep, the "B" word. But don't worry, we're not talking about restriction; we're talking about empowerment. A budget is your financial GPS, helping you navigate the road ahead. It's about aligning your spending with your values and priorities and discerning what can be savings, investments, and what you can use for life. Later on, we'll see how best to allocate your income in these categories.

- **Explore retirement accounts:** Peek into your retirement savings accounts. Are you contributing regularly? If not, consider boosting those contributions. If you're unsure about where to start, a financial advisor can be a fantastic ally in this adventure. It is like a doctor's advice–always be cautious and get a second opinion from someone like an accountant and or a financial advisor (but don't tell them that you already have advice; they almost always try to sell stuff...).

- **Social Security savvy:** Understand your Social Security benefits. When can you start claiming them? What impact will it have on your overall financial picture? It's like unlocking a treasure chest– you've earned it; now make the most of it.

- **Emergency fund:** Life happens, and a well-padded emergency fund can be your safety net. It's like having an umbrella on a rainy day–you might not need it often, but when you do, it's a game-changer.

Remember, this is about progress, not perfection. As you assess your financial readiness, celebrate the wins, and see the areas for growth as exciting opportunities. Think of it as tuning up your financial engine for the grand adventure of retirement

Retirement Savings and Investment Options: Navigating the Financial Landscape

Now that we've laid the groundwork for financial wellness, let's set our sights on the thrilling world of retirement savings and investment options. Think of it as choosing the colors for your canvas–this is where the magic happens, where your financial future transforms from a blueprint into a vibrant masterpiece.

Understanding Retirement Accounts

Ever heard of the phrase "Don't put all your eggs in one basket"? Well, that's our guiding principle as we explore retirement savings options. Diversification is the key, my friends! Let's break down some common retirement accounts:

- **401(k) and 403(b) plans:** If your employer offers one of these, consider it a gift from your future self. These plans allow you to stash away a portion of your paycheck before taxes, and some employers even throw in a dash of free money through matching contributions. It's like having a financial fairy godparent!

- **Traditional and Roth IRAs:** Individual Retirement Accounts come in two main flavors–traditional IRAs offer tax-deductible contributions, while Roth IRAs give you tax-free withdrawals in retirement. Choose the one that aligns with your current and future financial goals.

- **Health Savings Account (HSA):** An HSA isn't just for medical expenses—it can moonlight as a retirement superhero. Contributions are tax-deductible, grow tax-free, and withdrawals for qualified medical expenses are tax-free. Triple tax advantage? Yes, please!

Dabbling in Investments

Now, let's talk about investing; it's like planting seeds today to harvest a bounty in the future. Here's a quick rundown:

- **Stocks:** Think of stocks as ownership slices of companies. They can be a bit wild at times, like a roller coaster, but historically, they've outpaced inflation and provided solid returns over the long haul.

- **Bonds:** Bonds are like lending money to governments or companies, and in return, they pay you interest. They're like the steady, reliable friend in your financial circle, offering stability to balance out the excitement of stocks.

- **Mutual funds and exchange-traded funds (ETFs):** These are like financial buffets, offering a diverse mix of stocks, bonds, and other assets. They're a great way to spread risk while enjoying the variety of the market.

- **Real estate:** Whether it's investing in physical properties or real estate investment trusts (REITs), real estate can be a powerful addition to your investment portfolio. It's like planting a garden that grows in value over time. I would suggest this path, rather than leaving money in the bank, for people who have a lot of money to invest.

Remember: Investing is a long-term game. It's not about timing the market but time *in* the market. If the ups and downs of the financial world make your head spin, a financial advisor can be your trusty co-pilot on this exciting journey.

As you sculpt your retirement savings and investment strategy, think of it as creating a symphony–each instrument (or investment) plays its unique role. It's not about picking the perfect tune but crafting a harmonious blend that suits your lifestyle and risk tolerance.

Creating a Sustainable Budget for Retirement Life

Creating a budget in your early stages (when you are still working) is the best thing you can do. It is never too early (or too late)!

Take your expenses that are essential (housing, utilities, groceries, and healthcare). This should give you around 55% of your income–you may have to cancel or give up some nonessentials, but try to get as close to the 55% as you can. Some of my essentials include taxes, phone bills, public transport, insurance, doctor bills, and gas.

Then you have 10% for investing (i.e., stocks–check out app.tykr.com and look at the education and courses on the site–it is worth every cent. I can say from personal experience that money spent on education is well spent and will increase your income in the long run). Put the money in another account and invest when you have around $1,000–less than that and it's not worth the fees.

Another 10% can go for education, best in a separate account each month. Education will enhance your legacy and your potential income.

Another 10% should go to long-term investments like a car or a new fridge–more expensive items you might not otherwise have budgeted for. It can also go toward vacations, but only after you have a cushion of at least three times your salary.

It's only fair that you have fun with 10% and do whatever you want with it.

Put 5% toward donations to any organization you wish to support. (I go with seasheperd.com because I like diving.) Just make sure the money is going where you want it to go, not to, say, administration costs. If you cannot afford to do this right now, then allocate that 5% where it's needed.

When I started my financial journey, 80% of my spending was for essentials. I cut back on subscriptions and other unnecessary expenses and came to 70%. A friend of mine got hers down 20%–from 85% to 65%. I am now on 45% of my income as essential cost, mostly because I spent money on education, which brought me more income. If you have debt, use the same principle to pay it back. It will feel amazing to be able to pay off your debts.

Understanding Your Retirement Lifestyle

Close your eyes for a moment and picture your ideal retirement day. What are you doing? Where are you? Who are you with? Now, let's translate that vision into numbers. Your budget shouldn't feel like a set of restrictions but, rather, a tool to bring your dreams to life.

- **Essentials:** Start with the must-haves: housing, utilities, groceries, and healthcare. These are the building blocks of your budget, ensuring a sturdy foundation for your retirement home.

- **Lifestyle choices:** What makes your heart sing? Travel, hobbies, dining out, or perhaps supporting a cause dear to you? Allocate funds for the things that add joy and fulfillment to your days.

- **Emergency fund:** We talked about it earlier, but let's reinforce its importance. An emergency fund isn't just a financial cushion; it's peace of mind. Set aside a chunk for life's unexpected plot twists.

- **Anticipate changes:** Your expenses might shimmy and shift in retirement. Some costs, like commuting, might vanish, while others, like healthcare or leisure activities, might take center stage. Account for these changes as you draft your budget.

Diversification and Risk Management in Investment Portfolios

Let's circle back to our financial garden and talk about diversification and risk management. Remember, our goal is not just growth but *sustainable and steady* growth. Here's how you can achieve that:

- **Diversify your investments.** Spread your investments across different asset classes—stocks, bonds, real estate. It's like not putting all your tomatoes in one basket; if one investment doesn't perform well, others can pick up the slack. Be sure to stick with areas you are familiar with, as you are likely to do better investing in those.

- **Rebalance Regularly.** Your portfolio is a living organism, and its needs change. Periodically rebalance your investments to ensure they align with your goals and risk tolerance. It's like tending to your garden—a little pruning here, a little nurturing there...

- **Understand risk tolerance.** Risk is like spice in cooking—some like it hot, and some prefer milder flavors. Understand your risk tolerance. Are you comfortable with market fluctuations, or do you prefer a more conservative approach? Your investment strategy should match your comfort level.

- **Stay informed.** You don't need a finance degree, but staying informed about market trends and economic shifts can help you make informed decisions. Think of it as checking the weather before planning a picnic: A little preparation goes a long way.

Retirement is not about pinching pennies; it's about spending with intention. Every dollar you spend should bring you closer to your vision of an ideal retirement. Purposeful spending is the secret sauce that turns a budget into a roadmap for a fulfilling life.

Leisure Activities and Lifestyle Design: Infusing Your Retirement With Enrichment

Now that we've mastered the financial side of retirement, it's time to paint the canvas of your life with vibrant strokes of leisure activities and lifestyle design. In retirement you want to craft a life that makes your heart sing, where every day feels like a celebration.

Designing an Enriching Retirement Lifestyle

Think of this phase as your grand showcase, your chance to curate experiences and activities that fuel your soul. You can make these decisions before retirement. In fact, it is easier to begin earlier and then dip into it when you are in retirement. Here's how to design a retirement lifestyle that's as diverse and rich as the colors of a sunset:

- **Passions and hobbies:** What lights a spark in your soul? Whether it's painting, gardening, learning a new language, or volunteering, retirement is the perfect time to give your passions a go.

- **Travel and exploration:** Pack your bags (if you want to) and set off on new adventures. Whether it's exploring far-off lands or discovering hidden gems in your own backyard, travel can infuse your life with excitement and new perspectives.

- **Health and wellness:** Prioritize your well-being. Stay active, nourish your body with wholesome foods, and savor each moment. Exercise, yoga, meditation, or simply taking peaceful walks–find what keeps your mind and body in harmony.

- **Community and social connections:** Retirement is an opportunity to cultivate deeper relationships in addition to staying in touch with your old friends and connections. Engage with clubs, community groups, or simply connect with friends over a cup of coffee.

Crafting a Fulfilling Daily Routine Post-Retirement

Routine? In retirement? Absolutely! But this time, it's a routine sculpted to your desires, not bound by the 9-to-5 grind. Here's how to craft a daily rhythm that sings to your heart:

- **Morning rituals:** Start your day with purpose. It could be a serene morning walk, sipping a favorite brew while reading, or practicing mindfulness. Create a morning routine that sets a positive tone for the day.

- **Pursue passions:** Lean in to your hobbies and interests. Dedicate time each day to nurture your creativity, whether it's painting, writing, gardening, or learning something new.

- **Stay active:** Incorporate physical activity into your routine. It could be yoga, a dance class, swimming, or simply taking regular walks in nature. Moving your body keeps the joy flowing–and helps to keep you healthy.

- **Connect and converse:** Social connections are the spice of life. Whether it's lunch with friends, joining a book club, or volunteering, engage with others and cherish meaningful conversations.

Travel and Exploration in Retirement: Unveiling New Horizons

Your golden years are an open road, winding through landscapes of opportunity and discovery. Here's how to make the most of your travel adventures:

- **Wanderlust unleashed:** Retirement is the perfect time to let your wanderlust run wild. Whether it's ticking off items from your bucket list, exploring cultural hotspots, or embracing the serenity of nature, let travel be a passport to new experiences.

- **Slow travel:** Consider the art of "slow travel." Rather than rushing through destinations, immerse yourself in the local culture, savoring the flavors, and truly soaking in the essence of each place.

- **Culinary adventures:** One of the most delightful aspects of travel is indulging in local cuisines. From street-food stalls to fine dining, let your taste buds dance through a gastronomic journey around the world.

- **Connect with locals:** The heart of any place is its people. Engage with locals, hear their stories, and build connections that transcend borders. It's these encounters that often become the highlight of your travel tales.

Engaging in Lifelong Learning and Personal Development

Retirement isn't a pause button; it's a chance to hit play on continuous learning and personal growth. Let's explore how to keep the flame of curiosity burning bright in this next section.

- **Online courses and workshops:** The internet is a treasure trove of knowledge. Try some online courses and workshops to explore new subjects, hone existing skills, or venture into uncharted territories.

- **Book clubs and discussions:** Joining a book club or discussion group opens the door to shared wisdom and diverse perspectives. It's not just about reading; it's about engaging in conversations that expand your horizons.

- **Creative pursuits:** Unleash your creative spirit. Whether it's painting, writing, music, or photography, pursuing creative endeavors adds a vibrant layer to your retirement canvas.

- **Physical and mental wellness:** Embrace activities that promote overall well-being. From yoga and meditation to brain games and puzzles, keeping both your body and mind active is a recipe for a fulfilling retirement.

Volunteering and Community Involvement

There's immense joy in giving back to the community and being part of something larger than yourself. Let's explore how volunteering and community involvement can add depth and purpose to your retirement.

- **Identify your passion:** What causes tug at your heartstrings? Whether it's environmental conservation, education, or supporting local charities, find a cause that resonates with you.

- **Local organizations:** Connect with local organizations and nonprofits. Your time and skills can make a significant impact on the lives of others, fostering a sense of fulfillment and community.

- **Mentoring and sharing expertise:** Your wealth of experience is a valuable asset. Consider mentoring or sharing your skills with others, whether it's through workshops, mentorship programs, or community initiatives.

- **Create a legacy of giving:** Volunteering is about more than the present; it's about leaving a positive mark on the future. Consider creating a legacy of giving by supporting causes that align with your values.

Fulfillment in Later Years: Cultivating Purpose and Meaning

Now, let's get to the heart of fulfillment in the later years. In retirement you can relax and enjoy leisure time, but you also want to; find meaning and purpose in each day. Join me as we uncover the gems of personal purpose and infuse your golden years with meaning.

Defining Personal Purpose

- **Unveiling your unique path:** Your purpose is the compass that guides your journey. It's not a destination but a way of being. Let's try to uncover your unique purpose in this phase of life.

- **Reflecting on life's chapters:** Reflect on the chapters of your life. What experiences, triumphs, and challenges shaped you? Often, patterns emerge, guiding you toward your true calling.

- **Identifying passions and values:** Your passions and values are the pillars of your purpose. What activities light a spark in your soul? What principles do you hold dear? These are clues to your purpose.

Reflective Exercises to Uncover Passions and Values

- **Journaling journey:** Grab a pen and paper. Jot down moments in your life when you felt most alive, fulfilled, or deeply engaged. What were you doing? How did it align with your values?

- **Vision-boarding:** Get creative! Collect images, quotes, and symbols that resonate with you. Arrange them on a board to visually represent your aspirations and values.

- **Conversations and reflection:** Engage in deep conversations with trusted friends or family. Sometimes, an outside perspective can shed light on aspects of yourself that you might have overlooked.

- **Volunteer and explore:** Do more volunteer work or try new experiences. Sometimes, it's in the act of giving or trying something new that our purpose reveals itself.

Embracing Purposeful Living

Your purpose is your North Star, guiding decisions, actions, and the way you engage with the world. Embrace it with open arms, knowing that it's a compass that evolves with you.

- **Live your values.** Integrate your values into your daily life. Whether it's kindness, creativity, or environmental consciousness, let your values be the guiding principles in your choices.

- **Set goals with purpose.** Align your goals with your purpose. What aspirations contribute to your sense of fulfillment? Craft goals that nourish your soul and propel you forward.

- **Share your gifts.** Your purpose isn't just for you; it's a gift to the world. Whether through mentoring, volunteering, or simply being present for others, share your unique gifts.

Holistic Well-Being: Nurturing the Garden of Your Life

As we continue our exploration of later years, let's shift our focus to the intricate dance of holistic well-being. Your purpose, much like a garden, thrives when all aspects of your being–physical, mental, and emotional–

are tended to with care and intention. Join me as we uncover the art of nurturing your well-being in the golden phase of life.

The Interplay Between Physical, Mental, and Emotional Well-Being

- **Harmony in motion:** Finding fulfillment in later years is about nurturing and balancing the delicate combination of physical health and mental clarity.

- **Physical well-being:** Regular exercise, a balanced diet, and sufficient rest lay the foundation for a healthy body. Whether it's a brisk walk, gentle yoga, strength workouts, or embracing a new form of movement, prioritize activities that invigorate your physical well-being.

- **Mental sharpness:** Keep the gears turning with activities that challenge your mind. Engage in puzzles, learn new skills, or explore creative pursuits. Mental stimulation is the key to maintaining cognitive vitality.

- **Emotional resilience:** Embrace a full spectrum of emotions and cultivate resilience. Practices like mindfulness, meditation, or journaling can be powerful tools for understanding and managing emotions.

Importance of Self-Care Practices in Later Life

- **Listen to your body:** Your body is a wise companion. Pay attention to its signals and practice self-compassion. Adequate rest, relaxation, and regular health check-ups are acts of self-care.

- **Mindful nutrition:** Nourish your body with foods that support your well-being. Consider exploring a variety of nutritious options, and savor the joy of preparing and sharing meals.

- **Rest and relaxation:** Quality sleep is a cornerstone of well-being. Establish a soothing bedtime routine and create a sleep-friendly environment. Allow your body the rejuvenation it deserves.

Nurturing Relationships and Social Connections

- **Quality over quantity:** Cultivate meaningful connections with friends, family, and the community. It's not about the number of connections but the depth of the relationships that contribute to a rich and fulfilling life.

- **Shared activities:** Engage in shared activities that bring joy and connection. Whether it's a book club, a hiking group, or community projects, shared experiences create lasting bonds.

- **Communication:** Open, honest communication is the glue that holds relationships together. Express your thoughts, feelings, and appreciation regularly. It fosters a sense of connection and understanding.

Strategies for Managing Transitions and Changes in Later Years

- **Embrace change as growth.** Life is a series of transitions. Embrace them as opportunities for growth and adaptation. A flexible mindset allows you to navigate the ebb and flow of life with grace.

- **Seek support.** During times of change, don't hesitate to seek support from friends, family, or professionals. Sharing your thoughts and feelings can lighten the load and provide valuable insights. Go to more than one doctor. And, most important, don't take anything for granted–good and bad.

- **Create rituals.** Establish rituals that provide stability during transitions. It could be a daily practice, a weekly routine, or an annual tradition. Rituals anchor you amidst life's changes.

Giving Back and Philanthropy: Crafting a Legacy of Impact

Let's discuss giving back and philanthropy–a journey that transcends personal fulfillment to create a meaningful impact on society. As you explore ways to contribute, remember: Your legacy isn't just about what you accumulate; it's about the positive mark you leave on the world.

Volunteer Opportunities and Organizations

If you have already included this in your budget, good for you! Stick to it and, in retirement, you might have more time to devote to your cause.

- **Local initiatives:** Start close to home. Look for volunteering opportunities within your community. Whether it's supporting a local food bank, participating in environmental projects, or assisting at community centers, there are myriad ways to make a difference locally.

- **Global impact:** If you're feeling adventurous, consider volunteering on a global scale. Organizations like the Peace Corps or international NGOs provide opportunities to contribute your skills and passion to communities worldwide.

- **Skills-based volunteering:** Leverage your expertise. Many organizations welcome volunteers with specific skills. If you have professional experience, offer your knowledge to nonprofits or community groups.

Intergenerational Connections: Building Bridges Across Ages

Let's explore the beautiful world of intergenerational connections, sharing experiences and perspectives among different ages. These experiences are about learning, growing, and finding immense fulfillment in the diversity of human experience.

The Importance of Connection

- **Mutual learning:** Intergenerational connections create a conduit for mutual learning. Younger generations bring fresh perspectives, technological savvy, and enthusiasm, while older generations offer wisdom, life experiences, and historical context. It's a two-way street of knowledge exchange.

- **Emotional support:** Building relationships across generations provides emotional support. For younger individuals, guidance from older mentors can be invaluable. Likewise, older adults often find joy and fulfillment in guiding and supporting younger members of their community.

- **Reducing ageism:** By fostering connections, we break down stereotypes and reduce ageism. When different generations interact, they witness the richness and diversity of experiences that span a lifetime, challenging misconceptions about aging.

Benefits of Maintaining Relationships Across Different Age Groups

- **Diverse perspectives:** Engaging with individuals of different ages opens doors to diverse viewpoints and approaches to life's challenges. This diversity enriches your own perspective, fostering creativity and innovation.

- **Mutual support:** Intergenerational relationships create networks of support. Older individuals may provide guidance and mentorship, while younger ones offer technological expertise or fresh ideas.

- **Cultural exchange:** Each generation brings its unique cultural background and experiences. Through intergenerational connections, traditions are passed down, and cultural heritage is preserved and celebrated.

- **Building stronger communities:** Communities thrive on intergenerational connections. When people of all ages come together, it creates a sense of belonging and a shared responsibility to nurture the community's well-being.

Building Bridges: Strengthening Intergenerational Bonds

Establishing and nurturing connections across generations is like tending to a garden—it requires care, patience, and a willingness to cultivate meaningful relationships. Let's explore practical ways to foster and sustain these invaluable connections:

- **Engage in active listening.** Listen with an open heart and mind. Be genuinely interested in the stories, experiences, and perspectives of younger individuals. Show curiosity and ask questions that demonstrate your eagerness to understand their world.

- **Share your stories.** Offer glimpses into your own life experiences. Share stories about your youth, your challenges, triumphs, and the lessons learned along the way. Personal anecdotes create bridges of understanding and often spark intriguing conversations.

- **Embrace technology.** Don't shy away from technology; instead, embrace it as a tool for connection. Learn about social media platforms, texting, or video calls. Connecting through technology can bridge geographical distances and bring generations closer.

- **Seek common ground.** Find activities or interests that both you and younger individuals enjoy. Whether it's a hobby, a shared love for a particular sport, cooking, or art, engaging in activities together fosters camaraderie and strengthens bonds.

- **Be open to learning.** Be willing to learn from younger generations. They bring fresh perspectives, technological expertise, and innovative ideas. Embrace the opportunity to expand your horizons and acquire new knowledge.

- **Volunteer together.** Engaging in volunteer work or community service together creates a shared sense of purpose. It's a fantastic way to bond while making a positive impact on the community.

- **Respect differences.** Generational gaps might lead to differing opinions or approaches. Embrace these differences with respect and understanding. Acknowledge that diversity in viewpoints enriches the connection.

- **Be present and available.** Show your availability and willingness to connect. Offer support, guidance, and encouragement when needed. Being present in their lives demonstrates your commitment to the relationship.

- **Celebrate traditions and create new memories.** Share traditions from your generation while also being open to creating new experiences and memories together. Blend the old and the new to build unique bonds.

- **Maintain consistent communication.** Stay in touch regularly. A simple message, a phone call, or planning regular meetups helps nurture and strengthen relationships over time.

Remember, building bridges across generations is a journey, not a destination. It's about fostering connections that evolve, deepen, and bring immeasurable joy and enrichment to your life and theirs.

As we step into the next chapter of life, it's crucial to envision the possibilities and purposeful endeavors that await us beyond retirement. This is a phase brimming with opportunities to make a lasting impact on the environment, future generations, and, most importantly, on our own well-being.

Life After Retirement: A Wealth of Possibilities

- **Environmental stewardship:** Consider the legacy you wish to leave for future generations. Embrace a mindset of environmental stewardship. Whether it's reducing your carbon footprint, supporting sustainable practices, or engaging in conservation efforts, every action counts in preserving our planet.

- **Impactful relationships:** Beyond familial ties, cultivate meaningful connections with friends, neighbors, and the wider community. These relationships contribute to a plethora of shared experiences and mutual support, creating a legacy of interconnectedness.

- **Lifelong learning:** The pursuit of knowledge knows no age limit. Lifelong learning is a potent tool for staying engaged and purposeful. Enroll in courses, attend workshops, or explore topics that ignite your curiosity. The journey of learning never ends.

Guidance on Navigating Life Transitions Gracefully

- **Embrace change.** Life is a series of transitions. Embrace change with an open heart, acknowledging that each transition brings new opportunities for growth and discovery.

- **Re-evaluate goals.** Aspirations and goals evolve. Regularly assess and adapt your goals to align with your current passions and values. This flexible approach ensures that your journey remains purposeful and fulfilling.

- **Develop resilience.** Life's twists and turns can be unpredictable. Cultivate resilience by viewing challenges as opportunities for learning, adapting, and becoming more resilient in the face of adversity.

Advocacy for Lifelong Learning and Staying Engaged

- **Cultivate curiosity.** Curiosity is the fuel for lifelong learning. Stay curious about the world around you. Whether it's exploring new hobbies, delving into literature, or mastering a new skill, let curiosity be your guiding light.

- **Be a mentor and share knowledge.** As you accumulate wisdom, consider becoming a mentor. Share your experiences, offer guidance, and contribute to the growth of younger generations. The exchange of knowledge creates a legacy of wisdom.

- **Volunteer for educational initiatives.** Contribute to educational initiatives within your community. Support schools, libraries, or adult education programs. Your involvement can make a profound impact on others' learning journeys.

Beyond retirement lies a canvas waiting to be adorned with purposeful strokes. Whether it's making a positive impact on the environment, cultivating impactful relationships, or advocating for lifelong learning, each choice contributes to the legacy you leave behind.

Chapter 7:

Beauty Tricks for Sustainable

Aging

When it comes to aging, our society often throws around phrases like "timeless beauty" or "anti-aging secrets." But let's take a step back and ponder: What does beauty really mean when it comes to getting older?

Think about it. Beauty isn't a static concept—it's fluid, evolving with time, experiences, and wisdom. As we elevate the journey of aging, it's crucial to challenge the conventional standards of beauty that the world often imposes on us. It's about time we rewrite the rulebook and redefine what it truly means to be beautiful as we grow older.

Sure, there are countless creams, serums, and procedures out there promising to turn back the clock. And while there's nothing wrong with wanting to look and feel our best, there's so much more to the equation than just erasing a few wrinkles.

Age-defying beauty isn't merely about erasing lines or covering up those laugh crinkles (which, by the way, are absolute badges of joy earned through years of laughter). It's about nourishing ourselves inside and out, embracing our unique features, and radiating that inner sparkle that comes from a life well-lived.

The Aging Skin

Our skin is a remarkable canvas that tells the story of our journey through life. It's incredible how it evolves with us, mirroring the laughter, the tears, the sunny days, and the stormy ones. But, yes, it does undergo changes as we age. Understanding these changes is the first step to nurturing it the best way possible.

Let's talk science without getting too technical, shall we? Picture collagen as the scaffolding that supports our skin. It's like the invisible superhero responsible for keeping everything firm and supple. As the years roll by, this superhero begins to take a bit of a sabbatical, leading to a decrease in collagen production. The result? Wrinkles, fine lines, and a subtle loss of that youthful plumpness.

Elasticity, another buddy in the skin resilience team, also takes a hit. Think of it as the rubber band that stretches and snaps back into place. Over time, this rubber band can lose its bounce, leading to sagging and a lack of that once-firm tone.

And then there's pigmentation, those delightful sun- and age spots. While they tell stories of days spent under the sun, they also add character to our complexion. But understanding these changes doesn't mean we have to wave the white flag. Quite the opposite—we're gearing up for a beauty revolution.

Holistic Beauty Approach

Enter the concept of holistic beauty—a philosophy that embraces the beautiful interconnection between our internal well-being and external care routines. It's like a symphony where the harmony between what we put inside our bodies and how we treat the outside reflects in our overall radiance.

It's not just about slathering on the trendiest cream or getting the latest spa treatment. It's about the food on our plate, the joy in our hearts, the restful sleep we get, the laughter shared with friends, and the genuine care we give ourselves.

Imagine this: glowing skin that radiates from within, not just because of some serum but because of the nourishment we give our bodies through wholesome foods, hydration, and a lifestyle that feeds our soul.

We'll explore external skincare routines; we'll also uncover the magic of antioxidants, the wonders of hydration, the power of mindfulness, and the importance of a good night's sleep.

This holistic approach is about more than vanity—it's about honoring our bodies, appreciating the vessel that carries us through this beautiful journey called life, and giving it the love and care it deserves. So, get ready to explore a world of age-defying beauty that will find you embracing, nurturing, and enhancing the incredible canvas of your aging skin.

Every morning, when you look in the mirror, remind yourself that this beautiful face has been through life, and you can see all the beauty in this life in your reflection.

Sustainable Beauty Routines

Now that we've laid the foundation for a holistic approach to age-defying beauty, let's learn about some sustainable beauty routines. These are not quick fixes but lifelong practices that celebrate the beauty of aging in a way that's not only kind to your skin but also to the planet.

Skin Nutrition

Think of your skin as a reflection of what you put on your plate. You want–perhaps need–to feed your skin from the inside out. Skin nutrition is like a love letter to your body, expressing care through the foods you choose.

So, why is nutrition so crucial for maintaining healthy skin? Well, imagine trying to build a sturdy house with subpar materials—it wouldn't withstand the test of time. Similarly, your skin needs the right nutrients to stay resilient, elastic, and vibrant.

Let's talk about these superhero nutrients that can work wonders for our skin:

- **Vitamin C:** The powerhouse that boosts collagen production and fights off those pesky free radicals. Say hello to citrus fruits, strawberries, and bell peppers!

- **Vitamin E:** The protector that helps maintain skin health and shields against damage. Find it in almonds, spinach, tea, and sunflower seeds.

- **Omega-3 fatty acids:** The hydrators that keep our skin supple and glowing. Think salmon, flaxseeds, and walnuts.

- **Antioxidants:** The defenders against oxidative stress, found in berries, dark chocolate (yes, you read that right!), and green tea.

- **Resveratrol and collagen:** Anti-aging supplements that you'll want to look at and consider taking.

But just as there are foods to enjoy, there are also foods to avoid. Excessive sugar and processed foods can wreak havoc on our skin, leading to inflammation and breakouts. So, while that slice of cake might be tempting, your skin might thank you more for that handful of berries.

Hydration and Skin Vitality

Let's talk about the magic of hydration—our skin's best friend! Picture hydration as the life force that keeps our skin plump, elastic, and oh-so-radiant. It's like giving your skin a refreshing drink of water from the inside.

When we talk about skin elasticity, think of hydration as the secret sauce that maintains it. Our skin loves to be well-hydrated; it thrives on it. Hydration helps in maintaining that youthful bounce, minimizing the appearance of fine lines, and giving our skin that enviable glow.

Dehydration, on the other hand, can leave your skin looking tired, dull, and prone to wrinkles.

Now, how do we ensure our skin stays hydrated, especially as we age? It's not just about chugging gallons of water (though staying hydrated is crucial). We can also lock in moisture by using hydrating serums, moisturizers packed with hyaluronic acid, and incorporating foods with high water content into our diet—cucumbers, watermelon, and tomatoes, to name a few. You can also use retinol (an anti-aging cream), sunscreen (every day!), and whatever hydrating cream you already use.

Oh, and here's a fun tip: Try using a humidifier in your room to add moisture to the air, especially during those dry months. Your skin will thank you for creating a mini-oasis of hydration.

Sleep and Skin Rejuvenation

Next, let's talk about another rejuvenating ritual: sleep. Have you ever noticed how your skin seems to glow after a restful night? That's not a coincidence. Quality sleep is like a reset button for your skin, allowing it to repair and regenerate.

During deep sleep, our body releases growth hormones that stimulate cell turnover and collagen production, the dynamic duo for keeping our skin firm and youthful. On the flip side, poor sleep can lead to increased stress hormones, causing inflammation and, you guessed it, potential skin issues.

So, how do we optimize our sleep for healthier skin? Start by creating a calming bedtime routine—maybe a warm bath, some light reading, or gentle stretching. Limit screen time before bed to avoid disrupting your circadian rhythm, and ensure your sleep environment is cool, dark, and comfortable.

Consistent sleep patterns and adequate rest are like a magic wand for your skin, making sure you wake up not just feeling refreshed, but looking rejuvenated, too.

Stress Reduction and Skin Health

Stress is the silent villain in our quest for healthy, glowing skin. You see, stress isn't just a mental weight—it can also take a toll on our skin, affecting its health and radiance. But fear not, because managing stress is like giving your skin a deep breath of fresh air.

When stress comes knocking, it brings along a gang of hormones that can trigger inflammation, leading to a cascade of skin issues. Acne, eczema, and even premature aging can be linked to chronic stress. So, managing stress isn't just good for your mind; it's a gift to your skin, as well.

Stress-Relieving Techniques and Their Impact on Skin

You'll want to learn about the treasure trove of stress-relieving techniques that can become your skin's best friends. We discussed this more in detail in Chapter 5.

- **Mindfulness meditation:** Take a few minutes each day to simply breathe, centering yourself in the present moment. Mindfulness not only soothes the mind but also has a positive impact on the skin, promoting a healthy glow.

- **Yoga and gentle exercise:** Engage in activities that not only keep you physically active but also calm the mind. Yoga, in particular, has been shown to reduce stress hormones and promote overall well-being.

Let's zoom in on a delightful aspect of yoga that often gets overlooked but can work wonders for your skin—face yoga. It's like a little workout for the muscles of your face, promoting circulation, reducing tension, and enhancing that radiant glow.

The Beauty of Face Yoga

Face yoga involves a series of exercises designed to tone and relax the muscles in your face and neck. It's a natural way to combat the signs of aging, reduce stress held in facial muscles, and bring a refreshing lift to your features.

Top Three Face Yoga Exercises

1. The Lion Face:

   a. Sit comfortably and take a deep breath.

   b. Open your eyes wide, stick out your tongue, and stretch your fingers wide, like claws.

   c. Hold this pose for a few seconds, feeling the stretch in your face.

   d. Release with a deep exhale. Repeat a few times.

   e. The Lion Face is fantastic for releasing tension in the jaw and facial muscles, helping to reduce stress lines.

2. The Cheek Lifter:

   a. Smile as wide as you can without showing your teeth.

   b. Use your fingers to lift your cheeks toward your eyes, resisting the movement with your facial muscles.

   c. Hold for a few seconds, then relax.

   d. Repeat several times.

   e. The Cheek Lifter is perfect for toning the muscles around your cheeks and preventing sagging.

3. The Forehead Smoother:

a. Place your fingers on your forehead, spreading them out.

b. Gently sweep your fingers outward, applying light pressure.

c. As you reach the temples, lift your fingers and repeat.

d. Continue for a minute or two.

e. The Forehead Smoother helps alleviate forehead lines and releases tension in the forehead and scalp.

Just like any exercise, consistency is key. Aim for a few minutes of face yoga each day, perhaps as a part of your morning or evening routine. Not only will it contribute to stress reduction, but it's also a delightful self-care practice that connects your mind and body.

More Stress-Relieving Techniques

- **Aromatherapy:** Treat yourself to the power of scents. Essential oils such as lavender, chamomile, and rose can work wonders in creating a serene atmosphere, promoting relaxation.

- **Disconnecting from technology:** While technology is a marvel, it can also be a stress-inducing culprit, especially before bedtime. Take some time away from screens before bed, allowing your mind to unwind naturally.

  o You can make a plan for when you'll look at your phone, answer messages, and scroll through some apps. (I think there are phones that support such functions.) I told my friends and family that I am available only 6–8 p.m. and weekends 4–6 p.m. This is a game changer! The rest of the day my phone is silent. And I did the same with emails—when the time is up, I do not answer any more email. Sometimes it solves problems on its own. And for emergencies? I tell people to call and leave a short message—not longer than 20 seconds—which works perfectly. With a short message I can decide quickly what I need to do.

- **Quality time with loved ones:** The joy of connection is unparalleled. Spending time with loved ones, be it family, friends, or pets, releases oxytocin—the love hormone—which acts as a natural stress buster. You can even make an appointment with yourself or loved ones.

By incorporating these stress-relieving techniques into your routine, you're not just investing in mental well-being but also giving your skin a break from the detrimental effects of stress.

Science vs. Myths in Skincare

Now that we've journeyed through the realms of holistic beauty, skin nutrition, and stress management, let's set the record straight on some skincare myths. It's time to separate fact from fiction and ensure that your skincare routine is backed by science rather than hearsay.

- **Myth #1: Expensive products are always better.** Contrary to popular belief, the effectiveness of a skincare product isn't solely determined by its price tag. Ingredients matter more than the brand. Look for products with scientifically proven components like retinol, hyaluronic acid, and antioxidants, which can genuinely benefit your skin.

- **Myth #2: You can "shrink" pores.** Pore size is mostly genetically determined, and while you can't change their actual size, you can minimize their appearance by keeping them clean and using products that promote skin elasticity.

- **Myth #3: Natural means safe.** While many natural ingredients are fantastic for the skin, not everything from nature is a skin-friendly solution. Poison ivy is natural, but you wouldn't want that in your skincare routine! Always check ingredients and patch-test new products.

- **Myth #4: More products equal better results.** Quality beats quantity in skincare. Having a simple routine with effective products tailored to your skin's needs is far more beneficial than overloading your skin with multiple products that might counteract one another.

- **Myth #5: Sunscreen is only for sunny days.** UV rays are present even on cloudy days, and they can penetrate windows. Wearing sunscreen daily is your best defense against premature aging and skin cancer.

- **Myth #6: Aging skin can't look radiant.** Age is just a number, and radiant skin knows no bounds. A well-nourished, hydrated, and cared-for complexion can glow at any age.

Skincare is a blend of science and self-care. It's about understanding your skin's unique needs, choosing products with evidence-based ingredients, and developing a routine that suits you. Forget the myths; let's focus on what truly works for age-defying beauty.

So, the next time someone tells you a skincare secret passed down from generations or swears by a product that promises to turn back the clock, take a moment to separate the myths from the facts. Your skin deserves the best, and that begins with informed choices rooted in science. Besides, if what you are using is working, stick with it. Switching from lotion to lotion doesn't do your skin any good.

Now that we're diving deep into evidence-based skincare practices, let's uncover some tried-and-true methods backed by scientific research. These practices aren't just trends or fads; they're the real deal when it comes to nurturing your skin for sustained vitality and radiance.

Effective Skincare Routines Backed by Scientific Studies

- **Cleansing matters:** The foundation of any skincare routine is a clean canvas. Scientific studies emphasize the importance of gentle cleansing to remove dirt, pollutants, and makeup without stripping the skin of its natural oils.

- **Sun protection is non-negotiable:** Here's a fact backed by countless studies: Sunscreen is your skin's best friend. Daily use of broad-spectrum sunscreen with an SPF of 30 or higher helps prevent premature aging, sunburns, and skin cancer. Plus, it's anti-aging!

- **Retinoids, the anti-aging warriors:** Research consistently highlights the effectiveness of retinoids in reducing fine lines, wrinkles, and improving skin texture. These Vitamin A derivatives stimulate collagen production and promote cell turnover.

- **Hydration isn't just external:** Studies show that maintaining optimal skin hydration isn't just about slathering on moisturizer—it's about internal hydration, too. Drinking water helps maintain skin elasticity and overall skin health.

- **Antioxidants for skin defense:** Scientific evidence suggests that antioxidants, like Vitamin C and E, protect the skin from free radical damage caused by environmental stressors, leading to a brighter, more youthful complexion.

- **Consistency is key:** Perhaps the most underrated aspect backed by research is consistency. Studies emphasize the importance of sticking to a skincare routine to see tangible results. Patience and persistence pay off.

The beauty of these evidence-based practices is their adaptability. Tailor them to your skin type and concerns, ensuring you're nurturing your skin with what truly works.

Consider incorporating these practices into your daily routine, allowing science to be your guide in achieving radiant, healthy skin. Remember, it's not about quick fixes; it's about sustainable habits rooted in science that pave the way for timeless beauty.

Understanding Product Claims

Now that you're armed with science-backed skincare practices, let's navigate the often-confusing world of product claims and ingredient lists. It's like decoding a secret language that holds the key to effective skincare. Understanding what those labels really mean empowers you to make informed choices for your skin's well-being.

- **Beware of buzzwords.** Skincare products love catchy phrases, but not all are created equal. Terms like "all-natural," "organic," or "chemical-free" don't always guarantee effectiveness. Focus on specific ingredients rather than falling for marketing jargon.

- **Check the ingredient list.** This is where the magic happens. Ingredients are listed in descending order of concentration. If a key ingredient is near the end, it may not be potent enough to deliver on its promises. Look for proven ingredients like retinol, hyaluronic acid, and antioxidants.

- **Understand concentrations.** Some ingredients require a certain concentration to be effective. For instance, a product boasting Vitamin C might not do much if it contains a minimal amount. Research optimal concentrations for key ingredients to ensure you're getting the benefits.

- **Know your skin type.** What works for your friend might not work for you. Understanding your skin type and its specific needs helps in selecting products tailored to your skin's unique characteristics.

- **Fragrance matters.** While a pleasant scent can enhance the skincare experience, fragrance can be a potential irritant, especially for sensitive skin. Opt for fragrance-free or products with natural, nonirritating scents.

How to Navigate Product Labels for Effective Choices

- **Research key ingredients.** Before making a purchase, research the key ingredients in a product. Scientific studies and dermatologist recommendations can provide valuable insights into the efficacy of specific components.

- **Patch-test new products.** To avoid potential reactions, patch-test new products on a small area of skin before applying them to your face. This simple step can prevent unwanted surprises and ensure compatibility with your skin.

- **Be skeptical of miracle claims.** If a product promises miracles or instant results, approach with caution. Sustainable improvements in your skin often take time and consistency, not overnight transformations.

- **Consult with professionals.** When in doubt, seek advice from skincare professionals. Dermatologists can guide you on products suitable for your skin type and address specific concerns.

Navigating product claims and labels may seem daunting, but armed with knowledge, you can make choices that align with your skincare goals. Remember, your skin is unique, and so should your approach be to choosing products that truly work for you.

Biohacking Beauty

As we look deeper into the world of skincare, let's explore the frontier of innovation: biohacking beauty. Biohacking isn't just a term reserved for tech enthusiasts; it's a groundbreaking approach to skincare that leverages cutting-edge techniques for maintaining youthful, vibrant skin. Get ready to discover the exciting realm where science meets beauty!

Innovative Skincare Techniques

- **Microcurrent technology:** Imagine a workout for your facial muscles, but without breaking a sweat. Microcurrent technology uses low-voltage electrical currents to stimulate and tone facial muscles, promoting a lifted and sculpted appearance.

- **LED light therapy:** The power of light extends beyond our vision. LED light therapy involves exposure to specific wavelengths of light, targeting various skin concerns. From reducing inflammation to stimulating collagen production, LED therapy is a versatile biohack for healthier skin.

- **Nanotechnology in skincare:** Think small—really small. Nanotechnology involves using microscopic particles to deliver active ingredients deep into the skin. This technique enhances the efficacy of skincare products, ensuring they penetrate where they're needed most.

- **Microneedling with radiofrequency (RF):** This biohacking technique combines microneedling—creating tiny punctures in the skin to stimulate collagen production—with the added benefit of radiofrequency. The heat from RF enhances collagen remodeling, leading to improved skin texture and firmness.

- **Light therapy and photobiomodulation:** Biohacking has embraced light therapy as a powerful tool for skin rejuvenation. Different wavelengths of light stimulate cellular activity, promoting collagen production, reducing inflammation, and improving skin texture.

- **Noninvasive skin treatments:** Biohacking explores noninvasive treatments like microcurrent therapy, radiofrequency, and ultrasound to stimulate collagen production and tighten skin, offering alternatives to more invasive procedures.

Biohacking in skincare isn't just about gadgets and gizmos; it's about leveraging cutting-edge technologies to optimize your skin's health and appearance. While some of these methods might still be in their early stages, they hint at a future in which personalized, high-tech skincare becomes the norm. These innovative methods not only address current skincare concerns, but also contribute to long-term skin health.

As you explore the possibilities of biohacking beauty, remember that each technique should be approached with understanding and consideration for your skin's individual needs. You want to embrace innovations that align with your beauty goals, not chase trends.

The Use of Telemedicine and Virtual Consultations for Personalized Skincare Advice

- **Accessibility and convenience:** Telemedicine breaks down geographical barriers, allowing individuals from remote locations to access top-tier skincare advice. No more waiting months for an appointment; virtual consultations offer timely support.

- **Tailored recommendations:** Through detailed online assessments and discussions, dermatologists can provide personalized skincare routines, considering your skin type, concerns, and lifestyle. It's like having a skincare plan designed just for you.

- **Timely follow-ups:** Whether it's monitoring progress or adjusting treatments, telemedicine allows for consistent follow-ups, ensuring your skincare regimen evolves with your skin's needs.

- **Time efficiency:** In our fast-paced lives, time is a precious commodity. Telemedicine saves you the commute and waiting-room time, ensuring that you get expert advice without disrupting your daily schedule.

Telemedicine in skincare isn't just about convenience; it's about democratizing access to expert advice and making personalized care more accessible than ever. As you venture into this realm, remember that the screen doesn't dilute the expertise—it enhances it.

Tech-Integrated Skincare Tools

Let's explore the exciting world of skincare gadgets and devices that are revolutionizing the way we care for our skin as we age. These innovative tools harness technology to enhance our skincare routines, providing a blend of science and convenience for maintaining healthy, glowing skin.

- **Facial-cleansing brushes:** These handy devices use oscillating or rotating bristles to deep clean your skin, removing impurities and promoting better absorption of skincare products. They offer a gentle exfoliation that leaves your skin feeling refreshed.

- **LED masks:** Light-emitting diode (LED) masks have gained popularity for their ability to target various skin concerns using different wavelengths of light. Red light promotes collagen production, blue light fights acne, and yellow light helps reduce inflammation. It's a great way to start the day.

- **Smart moisturizing devices:** These devices analyze your skin's hydration levels and dispense the right amount of moisturizer accordingly. They ensure that your skin gets the hydration it needs, precisely when it needs it.

- **Microcurrent devices:** Mimicking the effects of a professional facial, microcurrent devices use low-level electrical currents to stimulate facial muscles. This helps tone and firm the skin, reducing the appearance of fine lines and wrinkles.

How to Incorporate Tech-Driven Skincare Tools Into Daily Routines

- **Choose tools aligned with your goals.** Identify specific skincare concerns or goals you want to address. Whether it's improving circulation, enhancing product absorption, or combating signs of aging, select devices that align with your objectives.

- **Start slowly.** Introduce one tool at a time to understand its impact on your skin. Incorporating multiple devices simultaneously can be overwhelming and may not allow you to gauge the effectiveness of each.

- **Follow instructions carefully.** Every skincare tool comes with instructions for a reason. Whether it's duration, frequency, or specific usage guidelines, following instructions ensures that you maximize the benefits without risking any adverse effects.

- **Be consistent.** Like any skincare routine, consistency is key. Set realistic expectations and commit to incorporating your tech-driven tools regularly. Results often become more apparent with time and consistent use.

- **Integrate devices into your routine.** Incorporate these tools at suitable points in your skincare routine. For instance, facial rollers can be used after applying serums to aid in absorption, and LED masks can be part of your nighttime regimen.

Tech-integrated skincare tools are not just gadgets; they're partners in your skincare journey. By embracing these devices, you're inviting innovation into your daily routine, enhancing the effectiveness of your skincare efforts.

Conclusion

What a journey it's been! From understanding the intricate science of aging to uncovering the secrets of sustainable and healthy living, we've navigated through various facets of what it means to age well.

From understanding the intricate science of aging to discovering the vital role nutrition plays in our vitality; from the power of exercise in sustaining our energy to the profound impact of managing stress on our mental well-being, we've discovered the diverse facets that shape our aging process. Let's not forget the essential insights into managing chronic conditions, embracing purposeful living in retirement, and even discovering beauty tricks for sustainable aging. Each chapter has been a stepping stone toward a fuller, healthier, and more vibrant life.

Throughout this journey, the core messages have remained constant. The crux of healthy aging lies not in grand gestures but in the daily choices we make. It's in the salad we choose over the fries, the walk we take after dinner, the breaths we use to calm our minds, and the hobbies that ignite our passions.

Remember, aging gracefully isn't about the absence of wrinkles; it's about the presence of joy, vitality, and fulfillment in every stage of life.

As we conclude this journey together, I urge you to take these learnings to heart and integrate them into your life. Start small—maybe with a few tweaks to your diet or adding a brisk walk to your routine. Embrace stress-relieving practices, explore hobbies that bring you joy, and seek purpose in each day. Remember, it's the little changes that snowball into significant transformations.

And here's a little challenge: Make it a habit to write a small review of your journey in a journal. Share your successes, your hiccups, and the moments that took your breath away. Your words might just inspire someone else to embark on their own path to healthy aging.

Let your experiences be a testament to the effectiveness of these strategies. Share your journey, your successes, and even your challenges with others. By doing so, you not only solidify these practices in your own life, but you also inspire those around you to embark on their path toward healthy aging.

Oh, and a small favor—your reviews and experiences matter! They inspire others to take the leap toward vibrant aging. Your feedback will not only help others discover the benefits of this journey but also fuel my passion to continue spreading the message of healthy and purposeful aging.

In closing, remember that the path to healthy aging is not about perfection but about progress. Every step you take toward a healthier and more fulfilling life is a victory in itself. Here's to a future filled with vitality, joy, and the wisdom that comes with gracefully embracing the journey of aging.

References

Al Aboud NM, Tupper C, Jialal I. *Genetics, Epigenetic Mechanism.* [Updated 2023 Aug 14]. In: StatPearls [Internet]. Treasure Island (FL): StatPearls Publishing; 2023 Jan-. Available from: https://www.ncbi.nlm.nih.gov/books/NBK532999/

Andrews, A. F. (2023, May 24). *A guide to face yoga for a healthy, sculpted glow.* *Vogue.* https://www.vogue.com/article/what-is-face-yoga

Balagam, I., & Murden, K. (2023, November 7). *From solawave to NuFace, these are the best skin care tools for a lifted, sculpted appearance.* Vogue. https://www.vogue.com/article/best-beauty-tools

Berciano, S., Figueiredo, J., Brisbois, T. D., Alford, S., Koecher, K., Eckhouse, S., Ciati, R., Kussmann, M., Ordovas, J. M., Stebbins, K., & Blumberg, J. B. (2022). *Precision nutrition: Maintaining scientific integrity while realizing market potential.* Frontiers in Nutrition, 9. https://doi.org/10.3389/fnut.2022.979665

Bergens, O., Veen, J., Montiel-Rojas, D., Edholm, P., Kadi, F., & Nilsson, A. (2020). *Impact of healthy diet and physical activity on metabolic health in men and women: Study Protocol Clinical Trial (SPIRIT Compliant).* Medicine, 99(16), e19584. https://doi.org/10.1097/MD.0000000000019584

Blueprint for Healthy Aging - Ilsi india. (n.d.-a). http://ilsi-india.org/PDF/Conf.%20recommendations/Nutrition,%20Immunity%20and%20Health/Blueprint%20For%20Healthy%20Agingg.pdf

Cao, C., Xiao, Z., Wu, Y., & Ge, C. (2020). *Diet and Skin Aging-From the Perspective of Food Nutrition.* Nutrients, 12(3), 870. https://doi.org/10.3390/nu12030870

Carabotti, M., Scirocco, A., Maselli, M. A., & Severi, C. (2015). The gut-brain axis: interactions between enteric microbiota, central and enteric nervous systems. Annals of gastroenterology, 28(2), 203–209.

Chu B, Marwaha K, Sanvictores T, et al. Physiology, Stress Reaction. [Updated 2022 Sep 12]. In: StatPearls [Internet]. Treasure Island (FL): StatPearls Publishing; 2023 Jan-. Available from: https://www.ncbi.nlm.nih.gov/books/NBK541120/

Clark, K. (2023, December 18). *How to double your money.* Investopedia. https://www.investopedia.com/articles/stocks/09/five-ways-double-investment.asp

Dalal, A. (2023, May 31). *10 ways to lead a purposeful life in 2023.* Coggno. https://coggno.com/blog/10-ways-to-lead-a-purposeful-life-in-2023/

Deana. (n.d.). *Innovative trends and technology in beauty and skincare industry.* Innovation cloud. https://innovationcloud.com/blog/innovative-trends-and-technology-in-beauty-and-skincare-industry.html

Dr. Tasnuva Sarwar Tunna (2018) *Complementary and alternative medicinal approach to stress management.* Frontiers Drug Chemistry Clinical Res. 2: DOI: 10.15761/FDCCR.1000113

Dresler, M., Sandberg, A., Bublitz, C., Ohla, K., Trenado, C., Mroczko-Wąsowicz, A., Kühn, S., & Repantis, D. (2018). *Hacking the brain: Dimensions of cognitive enhancement.* ACS Chemical Neuroscience, 10(3), 1137–1148. https://doi.org/10.1021/acschemneuro.8b00571

Edermaniger, L. (2022, February 14). *9 lifestyle and Diet tricks for biohacking sleep and insomnia.* Atlas Biomed blog | Take control of your health with no-nonsense news on lifestyle, gut microbes and genetics. https://atlasbiomed.com/blog/biohacking-sleep-and-biohacking-insomnia-with-lifestyle-and-diet/

Effective workout programs for different fitness levels - gym coach's guide. White. (n.d.). https://goteamup.com/resources/effective-workout-program

Farage, M. A., Miller, K. W., Elsner, P., & Maibach, H. I. (2013). *Characteristics of the Aging Skin. Advances in wound care,* 2(1), 5–10. https://doi.org/10.1089/wound.2011.0356

Galiè, S., Canudas, S., Muralidharan, J., García-Gavilán, J., Bulló, M., & Salas-Salvadó, J. (2020). *Impact of Nutrition on Telomere Health: Systematic Review of Observational Cohort Studies and Randomized Clinical Trials.* Advances in nutrition (Bethesda, Md.), 11(3), 576–601. https://doi.org/10.1093/advances/nmz107

Galiè, S., Canudas, S., Muralidharan, J., García-Gavilán, J., Bulló, M., & Salas-Salvadó, J. (2020). *Impact of Nutrition on Telomere Health: Systematic Review of Observational Cohort Studies and Randomized Clinical Trials.* Advances in nutrition (Bethesda, Md.), 11(3), 576–601. https://doi.org/10.1093/advances/nmz107

Gotter, A. (2018, April 20). *4-7-8 breathing: How it works, how to do it, and more.* Healthline. https://www.healthline.com/health/4-7-8-breathing

Graubard, R., Perez-Sanchez, A., & Katta, R. (2021). *Stress and skin: An overview of mind body therapies as a treatment strategy in dermatology.* Dermatology Practical; Conceptual. https://doi.org/10.5826/dpc.1104a91

Hoshaw, C. (2022, March 29). *What mindfulness really means and how to practice.* Healthline. https://www.healthline.com/health/mind-body/what-is-mindfulness

Huang, M. Y., & Woods, H. (2020, November 23). *A dermatologist and a cosmetic chemist debunk 19 skin-care myths.* Business Insider. https://www.businessinsider.com/beauty-experts-debunk-19-common-skin-care-myths-2020-11?r=US&IR=T

Jaiswal, A. (2023, June 5). *10 things to do after early retirement.* LinkedIn. https://www.linkedin.com/pulse/10-things-do-after-early-retirement-anshuman-jaiswal/

Jeff Diamond, A. (2023, July 24). *4 steps that may improve your retirement readiness.* Paces Ferry Wealth Advisors. https://pacesferrywealth.com/4-steps-that-may-improve-your-retirement-readiness/#:~:text=Retirement%20Readiness%20Step%20%232%3A%20Build,expenses%2C%20assets%2C%20and%20debts.

Jiang, Y., Abiri, R., & Zhao, X. (2017). *Tuning up the old brain with new tricks: Attention training via neurofeedback.* Frontiers in Aging Neuroscience, 9. https://doi.org/10.3389/fnagi.2017.00052

Johnson, J. (2023, April 4). *Brain exercises: 22 ways to improve memory, cognition, and creativity.* Medical News Today. https://www.medicalnewstoday.com/articles/brain-exercises

Khan, Z., & Zadeh, Z. F. (2014). *Mindful eating and its relationship with mental well-being.* Procedia - Social and Behavioral Sciences, 159, 69–73. https://doi.org/10.1016/j.sbspro.2014.12.330

Konicar, L., Prillinger, K., Klöbl, M., Lanzenberger, R., Antal, A., & Plener, P. L. (2022). *Brain Stimulation for Emotion Regulation in Adolescents With Psychiatric Disorders: Study Protocol for a Clinical-Transdiagnostical, Randomized, Triple-Blinded and Sham-Controlled Neurotherapeutic Trial.* Frontiers in psychiatry, 13, 840836. https://doi.org/10.3389/fpsyt.2022.840836

Kurutas E. B. (2016). *The importance of antioxidants which play the role in cellular response against oxidative/nitrosative stress: current state.* Nutrition journal, 15(1), 71. https://doi.org/10.1186/s12937-016-0186-5

Levy, J. (2023, July 15). *7 face yoga exercises to try now.* Dr. Axe. https://draxe.com/beauty/face-yoga-exercises/

Longo, V. D., Di Tano, M., Mattson, M. P., & Guidi, N. (2021). *Intermittent and periodic fasting, longevity and disease.* Nature Aging, 1(1), 47–59. https://doi.org/10.1038/s43587-020-00013-3

Lotta, L. A., Abbasi, A., Sharp, S. J., Sahlqvist, A. S., Waterworth, D., Brosnan, J. M., Scott, R. A., Langenberg, C., & Wareham, N. J. (2015). *Definitions of Metabolic Health and Risk of Future Type 2 Diabetes in BMI Categories: A Systematic Review and Network Meta-analysis.* Diabetes care, 38(11), 2177–2187. https://doi.org/10.2337/dc15-1218

Mahaffey, K. (n.d.). *Functional training: Compound workouts for fitness.* NASM. https://blog.nasm.org/functional-training-compound-workouts

Martin, A. C., & Candow, D. (2019). Effects of Online Yoga and Tai Chi on Physical Health Outcome Measures of Adult Informal Caregivers. *International journal of yoga*, 12(1), 37–44. https://doi.org/10.4103/ijoy.IJOY_5_18

Maynard, C., & Weinkove, D. (2018). *The Gut Microbiota and Ageing.* Sub-cellular biochemistry, 90, 351–371. https://doi.org/10.1007/978-981-13-2835-0_12

Meserole, L. (2002). *Health Foods in anti-aging therapy: Reducers of physiological decline and degenerative diseases.* Advances in Phytomedicine, 173–180. https://doi.org/10.1016/s1572-557x(02)80024-1

Miller E. M. (2020). *Using Continuous Glucose Monitoring in Clinical Practice.* Clinical diabetes: a publication of the American Diabetes Association, 38(5), 429–438. https://doi.org/10.2337/cd20-0043

Ms. Kavyashree, By, dietician, Ms. K. a seasoned, Kavyashree, Ms., & dietician, A. a seasoned. (2023, July 22). *Unmasking skincare facts and myths: What you need to know.* Kolors Healthcare India. https://www.kolorshealthcare.com/blog/unmasking-skincare-facts-and-myths-you-need-to-know/

Newmann, K. D. (2023, August 17). What is biohacking and how does it work? *Forbes.* https://www.forbes.com/health/wellness/biohacking/

NHS. (n.d.). *Breathing exercises for stress.* NHS choices. https://www.nhs.uk/mental-health/self-help/guides-tools-and-activities/breathing-exercises-for-stress/

Niazi, A. K., & Niazi, S. K. (2011). Mindfulness-based stress reduction: a non-pharmacological approach for chronic illnesses. *North American journal of medical sciences,* 3(1), 20–23. https://doi.org/10.4297/najms.2011.320

Oyetakin-White, P., Suggs, A., Koo, B., Matsui, M. S., Yarosh, D., Cooper, K. D., & Baron, E. D. (2015). *Does poor sleep quality affect skin aging?* Clinical and experimental dermatology, 40(1), 17–22. https://doi.org/10.1111/ced.12455

Palma, L., Marques, L. T., Bujan, J., & Rodrigues, L. M. (2015). *Dietary water affects human skin hydration and biomechanics.* Clinical, cosmetic and investigational dermatology, 8, 413–421. https://doi.org/10.2147/CCID.S86822

Pandey, S. (2018). *Factors contributing of aging.* Handbook of Research on Geriatric Health, Treatment, and Care, 393–408. https://doi.org/10.4018/978-1-5225-3480-8.ch022

Prakash, R. S., De Leon, A. A., Patterson, B., Schirda, B. L., & Janssen, A. L. (2014). *Mindfulness and the aging brain: a proposed paradigm shift.* Frontiers in aging neuroscience, 6, 120. https://doi.org/10.3389/fnagi.2014.00120

Puterman, E., & Epel, E. (2012). *An intricate dance: Life experience, multisystem resiliency, and rate of telomere decline throughout the lifespan.* Social and personality psychology compass, 6(11), 807–825. https://doi.org/10.1111/j.1751-9004.2012.00465.x

Raghupathi, W., & Raghupathi, V. (2018). *An Empirical Study of Chronic Diseases in the United States: A Visual Analytics Approach.* International journal of environmental research and public health, 15(3), 431. https://doi.org/10.3390/ijerph15030431

Riscuta G. (2016). Nutrigenomics at the Interface of Aging, Lifespan, and Cancer Prevention. *The Journal of nutrition,* 146(10), 1931–1939. https://doi.org/10.3945/jn.116.235119

Rodan, K., Fields, K., Majewski, G., & Falla, T. (2016). *Skincare bootcamp: The evolving role of Skincare.* Plastic and Reconstructive Surgery - Global Open, 4(12S). https://doi.org/10.1097/gox.0000000000001152

Roy, R., de la Vega, R., Jensen, M. P., & Miró, J. (2020). *Neurofeedback for Pain Management: A Systematic Review.* Frontiers in neuroscience, 14, 671. https://doi.org/10.3389/fnins.2020.00671

Ruegsegger, G. N., & Booth, F. W. (2018). *Health Benefits of Exercise.* Cold Spring Harbor perspectives in medicine, 8(7), a029694. https://doi.org/10.1101/cshperspect.a029694

Salazar, J., Durán, P., Díaz, M. P., Chacín, M., Santeliz, R., Mengual, E., Gutiérrez, E., León, X., Díaz, A., Bernal, M., Escalona, D., Hernández, L. A. P., & Bermúdez, V. (2023). *Exploring the Relationship between the Gut Microbiota and Ageing: A Possible Age Modulator.* International journal of environmental research and public health, 20(10), 5845. https://doi.org/10.3390/ijerph20105845

Sayer, A. (2023, May 19). *How many exercise rest days should you take a week? it depends.* GoodRx. https://www.goodrx.com/well-being/movement-exercise/how-many-exercise-rest-days-a-week

Schneider, A. M., Özsoy, M., Zimmermann, F. A., Feichtinger, R. G., Mayr, J. A., Kofler, B., Sperl, W., Weghuber, D., & Mörwald, K. (2020). *Age-related deterioration of mitochondrial function in the intestine.* Oxidative Medicine and Cellular Longevity, 2020, 1–12. https://doi.org/10.1155/2020/4898217

Schwalfenberg G. (2006). *Omega-3 fatty acids: their beneficial role in cardiovascular health.* Canadian family physician Medecin de famille canadien, 52(6), 734–740.

Segal, T. (2023, July 1). *What is diversification? definition as investing strategy.* Investopedia. https://www.investopedia.com/terms/d/diversification.asp

Skin health. Linus Pauling Institute. (2023, January 3). https://lpi.oregonstate.edu/mic/health-disease/skin-health

Sturgeon J. A. (2014). *Psychological therapies for the management of chronic pain.* Psychology research and behavior management, 7, 115–124. https://doi.org/10.2147/PRBM.S44762

Sud, E., & Anjankar, A. (2022). *Applications of Telemedicine in Dermatology.* Cureus, 14(8), e27740. https://doi.org/10.7759/cureus.27740

Tamplin, T. (2023, July 12). *Retirement readiness: Definition, Key Components, & Planning.* Finance Strategists. https://www.financestrategists.com/retirement-planning/retirement-readiness/

Team, T. I. (2023, December 12). *Individual retirement account (IRA): What it is, 4 types.* Investopedia. https://www.investopedia.com/terms/i/ira.asp

Tsegaye, D., Yazew, A., Gedfew, M., Yilak, G., & Yalew, Z. M. (2023). *Non-Pharmacological Pain Management Practice and Associated Factors Among Nurses Working at Comprehensive Specialized Hospitals.* SAGE open nursing, 9, 23779608231158979. https://doi.org/10.1177/23779608231158979

U.S. Department of Health and Human Services. (n.d.). *Continuous glucose monitoring - NIDDK.* National Institute of Diabetes and Digestive and Kidney Diseases. https://www.niddk.nih.gov/health-information/diabetes/overview/managing-diabetes/continuous-glucose-monitoring

U.S. Department of Health and Human Services. (n.d.-a). *Four types of exercise can improve your health and physical ability.* National Institute on Aging. https://www.nia.nih.gov/health/exercise-and-physical-activity/four-types-exercise-can-improve-your-health-and-physical#:~:text=Endurance%20exercises%20improve%20the%20health,Brisk%20walking%20or%20jogging

U.S. Department of Health and Human Services. (n.d.-b). *Skin care and aging.* National Institute on Aging. https://www.nia.nih.gov/health/skin-care/skin-care-and-aging

Venegas-Carro, M., Herring, J. T., Riehle, S., & Kramer, A. (2023). *Jumping vs. running: Effects of exercise modality on aerobic capacity and neuromuscular performance after a six-week high-intensity interval training.* PLOS ONE, 18(2). https://doi.org/10.1371/journal.pone.0281737

Walker, M. (2017). *Why We Sleep: Unlocking the Power of Sleep and Dreams.* Scribner.

Watson, N. F., Badr, M. S., Belenky, G., Bliwise, D. L., Buxton, O. M., Buysse, D., Dinges, D. F., Gangwisch, J., Grandner, M. A., Kushida, C., Malhotra, R. K., Martin, J. L., Patel, S. R., Quan, S. F., & Tasali, E. (2015). Recommended Amount of Sleep for a Healthy Adult: A Joint Consensus Statement of the American Academy of Sleep Medicine and Sleep Research Society. *Sleep,* 38(6), 843–844. https://doi.org/10.5665/sleep.4716

What exercise is right for me?. www.heart.org. (2022, June 2). https://www.heart.org/en/healthy-living/go-red-get-fit/what-exercise-is-right-for-me#:~:text=Get%20at%20least%20150%20minutes,least%202%20days%20per%20week.

Wilkins, H. M., & Swerdlow, R. H. (2021). *Mitochondrial links between Brain Aging and Alzheimer's disease.* Translational Neurodegeneration, 10(1). https://doi.org/10.1186/s40035-021-00261-2

Wilson, B. (2023, July 18). *Understanding how to budget for retirement.* Hachette Australia. https://www.hachette.com.au/news/understanding-how-to-budget-for-retirement

Yu, B., Funk, M., Hu, J., Wang, Q., & Feijs, L. (2018). *Biofeedback for everyday stress management: A systematic review.* Frontiers in ICT, 5. https://doi.org/10.3389/fict.2018.00023

Zhang, B., Trapp, A., Kerepesi, C., & Gladyshev, V. N. (2022). *Emerging rejuvenation strategies-Reducing the biological age.* Aging cell, 21(1), e13538. https://doi.org/10.1111/acel.13538

Printed in Great Britain
by Amazon

57680581R00086